Take That Old Car Out of Your Front Yard and Plant a Garden!
By Arlene Wright-Correll

Original illustrations by Arlene Wright-Correll

Forward

The world is changing. The weather is changing. The cost of living is constantly changing and we daily try to keep up with all those changes. We add stress upon stress onto our lives and cannot seem to figure out why we are having heart attacks and cancer like never before.

What are we doing to change ourselves in order to deal with these changes or to relieve our stress? Well, take that old truck out of the front yard and make a garden! Don't want to plant a garden, plant an orchard, a forest or a Mediterranean herb garden.

It isn't hard. Start small, but start and start smart. This little book of 14 chapters will be a good starter book of information and tips for the novice gardener. My gardening books, like my gardens, ramble all over the place. However, the information in them might just be the thing to start you down the Primrose Path!

Should any of you ever be in our neck of the woods, please note that the latch string is always out. Currently we run Avalon Stained Glass School at 100 Dave Wintsch Rd. in Munfordville, KY 42765 and I am the resident artist and still the gardener. So come and see us and feel free to pick all the free weeds you can stuff in your trunk or at least visit us at www.learn-america.com

This book is dedicated to our grandchildren, Jennifer, Kane, Scott, Ryan and Andrew who hopefully will be strong enough to endure all the coming changes and find time in their busy lives to make a garden.

Cover painting by Arlene Wright-Correll "Abandonment©"
http://www.learn-america.com/stories/storyReader$1681

Copyright 2007
ISBN # 978-0-6151-5104-5
Publications Trade Resources Unlimited
100 Dave Wintsch Rd., Munfordville, KY 42765

Other books by this author can be found at http://stores.lulu.com/kate1031

The Bakers Dozen©
The Impractical Gardener©
Who's Who in KY Arts and Crafts© 2006 Edition

You can go on line and buy Arlene's Home Farm Flowers and we will ship you the freshest, least expensive flowers direct from the grower to you.

http://www.growerflowers.com/default.asp?id=37350

You can find Arlene's original art or Giclee prints of her works at
http://www.learn-america.com/stories/storyReader$158

Find information about Avalon Stained Glass School & Art Gallery at
http://www.learn-america.com/stories/storyReader$134

Deco Garden©

Chapter 1: How to Grow an Easy Flower Garden

Chapter 2:   How to Divide Daffodils

Chapter 3: Planting a Vegetable Garden

Chapter 4: How to know what trees to plant

Chapter 5: How to handle little garden problems

Chapter 6: How to Grow Columbines

Chapter 7: Some Thoughts about Flowers (from Azaleas to Lilacs and more, plus flower arrangements and other good gardening info)

Chapter 8: Do You Have a Witch Hazel Tree in Your Yard or Woods?

Chapter 9:   How to Divide Cannas

Chapter 10: How to Care for Crape Myrtle

Chapter 11:   How to Prune Flowering Shrubs

Chapter 12: Every Garden needs Deer Resistant Plants

Chapter 13: So You're Thinking of Planting an Apple Orchard

Chapter 14: Starting a Garden is like having a Baby!

Chapter 1

How to Grow an Easy Flower Garden

Gardening is hard work and anyone who says it isn't must know something I don't know. However, it is good exercise, frustrating, gratifying and many other things.

I love flowers and hate weeding so over the years I have tried to find some easy, colorful and reseeding flowers for my gardens. I like lots of bright jewel-like flowers such as poppies, cornflowers, hollyhocks and Love-in-a-mist and these are self seeding flowers that are easy to grow.

When you think about flowers just think about perennials and annuals. Perennials come back every year and annuals have to be planted each year. We also should include bi-annuals which come back every other year.

As an artist, I tend to think of the flowers in my garden as I would the colors on my palette. These seeds as they grow and bloom become my brush strokes in my gardens.

Foxglove is a biannual that forms the rosettes the first year and the purple flower spike the second year. This grows best in full sun to part shade. It also prefers nitrogen rich soil.

Blooms June - September
Height 2 - 4 feet
Sowing depth surface sow
Germination 2 - 4 weeks

I like **Black eyed Susan** as it is a very hardy perennial with yellow petals and a black domed center. Nothing stops it. This grows best in full sun. It is a very easy to grow flower and just lovely in your garden. It also is a nice cutting flower.

Blooms June- August
Height 2-3 feet
Sowing depth 1/16 inch

Germination 1-4 weeks.

Another easy to grow, favorite of mine is the **Shirley corn poppy.** It is just like the Flanders field poppy but in a mix of colors. The blooms are 3 to 4 inches across with red, white and pink flowers and it looks great when planted in mass.

Blooms March - July
Height 2 - 2 ½ feet
Sowing depth surface sow

Germination 1 - 4 weeks

Indian Spring Hollyhocks bloom with mostly single flowers in shades of rose, pink and white. These old-fashioned flowers grow 5 to 7 feet tall and are an excellent backdrop for shorter flowers in informal planting beds. Although a perennial, Indian Spring can bloom the first year if sown early. They can also be planted all summer long to bloom early the next year. Hollyhocks love the sun and heat. Space 4 inches apart to start with and thin to 2 feet apart once they have grown to 2 feet tall.

Blooms March- September.
Height 5-7 feet
Sowing depth 1/8 inch
Germination 2-4 weeks.

Bachelor's button is an annual with white, pink, red, and blue flowers and the one I especially like is the dwarf polka dot mix that grows to a height of 24 to 30 inches. These are my all time favorite. These flowers work great in flower arrangements or as a dried flower.

Blooms March - June
Height 2- 3 feet
Sowing depth 1/8 inch
Germination 1 - 3 weeks

Orange sulphur cosmos loves the heat and is drought tolerant and this is a very easy flower to grow. Not only do I love the color as it really jazzes up the garden, it also attracts birds and butterflies. Plus it is also great as a cut flower and it reseeds in warmer climates.

Blooms July - September
Height 1 - 2 feet
Sowing depth 1/16 inch
Germination 1 - 4 weeks

Dames rocket is a perennial with lilac-purple flowers. This flower gives off a wonderful aroma in the evening. It prefers full sun to partial shade. I plant mine on the edge of the rose arbor around my house and it looks very nice. Usually these seeds can not be shipped to Colorado.

Blooms May - August
Height2- 3 feet
Sowing depth 1/16 inch
Germination 3 - 4 weeks

Siberian wallflower is a perennial in warm climates and a biannual in colder climates. You should plant these seeds in part shade in warmer climates and in the sun in the cooler climates. This has many bunches of bright orange flowers on short bushy plants and the nice thing about it is it can withstand moist or dry conditions once established.

Blooms April - June
Height 1 - 1 ½ feet
Sowing depth 1/16 inch
Germination 2 - 4 weeks

White Yarrow is another wonderful perennial with clusters of white flowers and fern like foliage. Yarrow can handle just about anything. However, it requires full sun. Mixing in a patch of white yarrow here and there seems to spice up the color scheme in my garden and it will in yours also.

Blooms May - November
Height 1 - 3 feet
Sowing depth surface sow
Germination 3 - 6 weeks

Mexican Hat is a drought tolerant perennial. The flowers are bright red outlined with yellow with a long black cone in the center. They prefer full sun. This is also a great cut flower which will last up to 10 days. These are fun flowers that just perk up any garden.

Blooms June - September
Height 2-3 feet
Sowing depth 1/16 inch
Germination 2-5 weeks

Zinnias are my all time favorite annual flower as they come in all heights and are just brilliant in all kinds of colors.

Zinnia Lilliput mix is an annual that blooms quickly. Usually in 6 to 8 weeks after planting. It blooms until frost. These flowers bloom in yellow, white, pink, red, and orange. Zinnias are the easiest flower in the world to grow in my personal opinion.

Blooms May - frost
Height 1 ½- 2 feet
Sowing depth 1/8 inch
Germination 1 - 3 weeks

Red corn poppy is another great annual. It has 2- 4 inch bright red flowers with almost black centers. Also know as Flanders fields poppy. It grows best in full sun to partial shade.

Blooms March- July
Height 2- 2 ½ feet
Sowing depth surface sow
Germination 1-4 weeks.

Chinese houses are annuals that prefer partial shade with dry well drained soil. They have purple and white blooms that look like Chinese pagodas hence the name. They make a great border. However, it does not tolerate extreme heat. I think these are adorable and so unusual.

Blooms March - June
Height 1 ½- 2 feet
Sowing depth 1/16 inch
Germination 1 - 4 weeks

Love in the mist is an annual that will re seed every year on its own. Just plant the seeds in full sun and in well drained soil. White flowers are great for cut flowers and dried flowers. The seed pods look like little watermelons where the flower used to be.

Blooms June - August
Height 1 ½- 2 feet
Sowing depth 1/16 inch
Germination 1 - 3 weeks

Zinnia California giant mix is an annual with flowers nearly 5 inches across. These flowers are red, yellow, purple, white, and pink. As I have said before these plants are easy to grow and reach 3 feet in height. They make a great back border. Zinnias of any kind make great cut flowers and they will continue to produce if you keep dead heading them.

Blooms May - frost
Height 2 - 3 feet
Sowing depth ¼ inch
Germination 1 - 3 weeks

Candytuft is an annual with white, pink, and or lilac flowers that bloom most of the summer and into the fall. Theses work great as a border or in pots so if you are a container gardener, then this one is for you. It is also a good cut flower and attracts birds, bees and butterflies.

Blooms June - September
Height 1 - 1 ½ feet
Sowing depth 1/16 inch
Germination 3 - 4 weeks

Gloriosa daisy is an annual or short lived perennial. It has huge 4 to 9 inch yellow flowers with a brownish red tint on the petals as you get closer to the center cone of the flower. This flower prefers full sun and is heat and drought tolerant. Nothing stops it! You will find that as cut flowers they will last up to 2 weeks.

Blooms June - September
Height 2 - 3 feet
Sowing depth 1/16 inch
Germination 1 - 4 weeks

On another topic one should not forget bulbs. Buy good tulip, daffodil and other bulbs and take time each fall to plant your bulbs for next year before the first frosts.

To get the best results buy as high-quality bulbs as you can afford, make sure they have no bruises or soft spots or mould on them. They like a sunny spot and well drained soil. Remember that daffodils should be planted with the pointed end up at least 6 inches deep and if you can 8 inches. Don't forget to leave them room to grow and multiply so leave at least 3-5 inches between bulbs. They will flower year after year for you. Just remember that most of these flowers will need to have their dead leaves and stem there after the bloom has died. This is so all the plant food and energy will go back down to the bulb for next year. If you whack them off or trim them so your garden looks nice after the bloom in gone, you can forget about seeing those flowers next year.

Here are some planting tips for the Morning glory, perennial lupine and Moonflower seeds. Soak the seeds in water for 24 hours just before you plant them ¼ inch (morning glory and lupine) or 3/8 inch (moonflower) deep. Keep the soil moist until they are up a couple of inches and after that water when the topsoil looks dry. A good thing to remember about morning glories is to never put them where they can get at your other plants or they will chock them out. They will come back year after year, looking beautiful every morning, but they will raise havoc with any thing they can snake out to reach and twist their vines too. Think about where you are putting them. I put some in the wrong place and I spend a great deal of time taking them off my roses etc. They are coming back each year in the darndest places.

Blanket Flower seeds need sunlight to germinate so don't cover the Blanket Flower seeds completely with soil.

Seeds like Shirley corn poppy, red corn poppy, and foxglove and baby snapdragon are very small and should be sown on the surface of the soil. You can then roll them with a roller or walk on them to make sure they come in good contact with the soil. No additional soil on top of them is needed. Water gently so they don't get washed away. I sometimes cover mine with burlap to prevent this from happening from the rain. Remove the burlap as soon as they sprout.

Rocket larkspur seeds need darkness to germinate. Make sure you cover the rocket larkspur seeds with 1/8 inch of soil. If you are starting some in pots you can cover them with a piece of wood also.

Here are some planting tips for your seeds. To plant the seeds start by taking out whatever weeds and unwanted vegetation you have in the area. It is easier before you plant. Use roundup or pick them by hand. (Get all the roots) Remember, like flowers there are annual and perennial weeds. It is best to plant your seeds when the average temperature is 60 to 70 and just before the rainy season, usually spring in most of the country.

Don't till up the ground deeper than an inch if you can help it because it will bring up dormant weed seeds. Then put one pack of seeds in a container with about ¼ cup of sand. (Use 6 to 8 cups of sand for each pound of wildflower mix).This way you will be able to see where you are spreading them and get a larger area covered.

Keep sand and seeds mixed well at all times so they don't become separated. Throw out the seed by hand going over the area twice in two different directions. Keep mixing the seeds and sand. When you are done rake the seeds in lightly and walk over the area so the seeds come in good contact with the soil. You don't want the seed to go down in the soil any deeper than they are thick. There will be a lot of seeds on the surface. This is normal. Or you can plant them one at a time by hand. Then just keep the area moist until the plants come up.

Once the seeds germinate don't let the soil dry out before the plants come up a couple of inches or they will die. After the seeds have sprouted with leaves water them when they ground looks dry.

Once you have gotten the gardening bug you may want to think towards other things. Remember to keep your thinking simple. In the fall as the leaves start to fall it seems a shame to waste them and homemade leaf mould makes such great compost for the garden.

You can make a small amount in a black plastic sack or a large amount in a compost heap depending on your circumstances.

So if you are busy sweeping up leaves look upon them as free excellent compost for your garden. Should you not have any leaves, just find your neighbors with trees and watch as they blow them, bag them and put them out to their curb for trash pick up. Ask them if you may them. When they say yes, remember them each summer with a bouquet of beautiful flowers from you garden. They will enjoy them and be rewarded for sharing their leaves with you. You might also want to volunteer to sweep up for them in return for the leaves, especially if your neighbor is an older person.

Here is a recipe for making mulch of small amounts of leaves
First you need some black plastic waste bin liners
Next make some small holes in the bottom of the bin liners – taking care you don't make them too big (or cut yourself) – a small sharp object such as a knitting needle or skewer is fine.

Sweep up your leaves and pop them in your bag – you can do this over several days or weeks. When the bag is full add three pints of water and allow it to drain through.
Pack the leaves down tightly and tie bag top

Leave your bags in a corner somewhere out of the way for a year. Make sure they are somewhere safe – not anywhere a friend or partner will mistake them for rubbish - and put them out with the trash!

When you open them you will have an excellent mulch to put round your prize perennials. You can also use it to enrich your soil if you dig it in. I much prefer to use it as mulch one year and then it seeps into the soil without me having to dig it in!

If you can manage to leave your bags for two years the leaves will have rotted down so much that you will be able to use it as potting compost – not bad for free pickings!

Another leaf mould tip is you can add some grass cuttings to your leaves – add a good thick layer of leaves then a thin layer of grass cuttings then repeat twice.

If you have a shredder then you can shred the leaves before putting them in the bags – this will speed up the whole process.

So here you have the good start of an easy garden to grow. I would recommend any of these flowers for a good starter garden. Lay out a play where you want your garden to be. It would be prudent to draw it on paper and pencil in the places with the flowers names written on those areas.

Zen Poppies©

Chapter 2

How to Divide Daffodils

Living in zone 6 gives me the ability to consider lots of perennials and one of them is daffodils. Ever since we moved to Kentucky, we have never been here in the winter. We usually leave to follow the sun about mid November and come back about the end of April. By then most of the spring bulbs have come and gone. This is the first spring we have been here and it was an amazing delight to see all the different types of daffodils I had planted. I usually only get to see the green stems and leaves.

I remember the first year we moved here, I gave my daughter-in-law a present of about 100 tulip bulbs and 50 or so Daffodil bulbs. She planted them in the fall and they graced her entryway in the following spring. I mentioned to her that it was necessary to allow the tulips, once they lost their blossom, to get that scraggly, droopy look as tulips needed to have their strength or energy go back down towards the bulb in order to produce again and again. Needless to say, the first weed whacker job did them in and they were never to be seen again. However, the Daffodils did not get the "hatchet job" for some reason and they had bloomed every year in the same area since the spring of 1998. The weed whacker caught up with them the other day by my grandson before I could issue instruction, so who knows what will happen. These were just ready to be divided, as they were pretty tight in that one area. I doubt they will come back again next spring.

Daffodils are among the easiest and showiest bulbs to grow in the early flowering garden. They love lots of sun but tolerate a half-day shade. Yet, they grow just fine among deciduous trees because they flower before most trees leaf out. I love the daffodil because it is such an early harbinger of spring. It is sometimes referred to as a buttercup or a jonquil. These are all common names and they are all correct. But its Latin, or botanical name, is narcissus.

Over the years I have purchased daffodil bulbs that bloom at different times of spring. So it might behoove you to look at the blooming time when you purchase daffodil bulbs. They are usually labeled, early spring blooming, mid-spring blooming and late spring blooming. This gives me daffodils over a longer period of time.

Once the joy of the blooms have come and gone, one of the first questions that arises is what year you should treat it with respect. This grass like foliage actually restores the bulb's energy through photosynthesis. It helps it prepare for blooming next year so don't cut it back. It's okay to remove the spent flower but be sure to leave the stem intact. Even though the foliage begins to look a little scruffy let the foliage die back at least six weeks to rejuvenate the bulbs for next year's flowers. Divide daffodils every three to five years or when the bulbs produce few flowers.

Since daffodil blooms seem to be everywhere in the spring, I always thought they were Native American wildflowers, but they're not. Most of them come from Europe and have been used in gardens long before the time of the Romans. Over the years, many different varieties of daffodils have been developed. In fact, they are divided into twelve main divisions and numerous subdivisions, which help us to keep them straight.

One question has always stumped me. I will see daffodils planted in someone's yard. Then I see clumps of them nearby in the oddest places such as down the road in a ditch in a nice clump. I do not think they have been planted there. How did they get there? At any rate, let's get back to the theme of this chapter

Dig as soon as the foliage starts to die, but is still visible. Separate the bulbs in the clumps, but do not tear them apart as they will come apart when ready. Of course just remember the name of the game here is to keep the foliage green as long as possible. As long as the foliage is green it is working to recharge the bulb for next year's flower. You may damage them by tearing them apart if they are visibly attached; many bulbs stay in place for years and continue to bloom with proper fertilization. Feed bulbs in the fall; top-dress them with a slow-release 5-10-20 daffodil fertilizer. Greensand, bone meal and wood ashes from your fireplace make good organic nutrients.

However, if you don't periodically dig up and divide your daffodils, you'll find the bulbs are very small and won't produce as many flowers. Every year in Holland they dig up and sell their largest daffodil bulbs. I like to replant my largest bulbs where I like them to be seen and you could put the smaller bulbs in the back of your garden and fertilize them to encourage root growth. I like to start new beds with them, myself.

As I get older and have less strength, I have to find easier ways to garden. I have become the "cardboard box" gardener. I used to use weed block, but that does not break down. Cardboard boxes are not only biodegradable, they are cheaper and I love recycling stuff. I always like to make "rooms" for my garden or boarder beds in certain areas. Cardboard boxes work for me. I do not have to rotor-till the grass and all the hard work that goes with it. I just put down my boxes after I have broken them apart to make them flat. Newspapers work well also, but tend to fly around in the wind. Try to avoid the colored sections of newspapers as they usually have different chemicals in them. I lay my cardboard out larger than the area I am going to cover with dirt. That way I can lay an extra foot or so of mulch around the dirt and the mower person or weed-whacker person does not come near my bulbs or plants.

I also like raised beds as raised beds warm up quicker in the spring. After I have laid down my cardboard in the area I want the new bed, I engage my strong 16 year-old grandson at $5.00 per hour to haul my 40 pound bags of topsoil for me to the cardboard. This is usually done in an hour or less and worth every penny of the $5.00 bill. I use one bag of black cow to 4 bags of topsoil and he opens them up onto the cardboard. (Now that he has grown up and enlisted in the Navy, it is harder to find help even paying $8.00 an hour!)

It is into these raised prepared beds that I plant my Daffodil bulbs or any other plants or seeds I intend to plant. However, since this is an article about daffodil dividing we will now get to the five simple steps of doing so. Over the years, a single bulb can produce many offsets. Most small-flowered can continue to bloom when congested. The large-flowered daffodils suffer terribly when they become crowded and bear fewer, smaller blossoms or even none after 3 or 4 year. So you see dividing the clumps does the daffodil a big favor, besides giving you a nice supply of bulbs without the cost of buying them.

Step 1. As I said before, dig your daffodils in the summer just after the foliage ripens and dies down. The location of the bulbs will be apparent because you can still see when the foliage enters the ground. I like to use a flat garden fork to dig up large clumps of bulbs, as this tends to cause less damage to the bulb than a spade does. Always insert the fork in the soil several inches away from the bulb to avoid spearing them. Carefully pry out the clump of bulbs.

Step 2. Handle the bulbs gently as bruised bulbs tend to rot. Use your fingers to brush off excess soil. Most bulbs will separate naturally as the soil is shaken off. Other may remain connected at the bottom or basal plate. Gently break apart those that are loosely connected, leaving the offsets that are firmly attached to the mother bulb. Discard any bulbs that are soft, rotten, or damaged.

Step 3. Daffodil bulbs can be planted immediately or stored for fall planting. I always plant immediately as I have too many other things to do in the fall and I am too lazy to cure the bulbs in order to harden them and keep them better. However, should you wish to do so, set an old window screen on two boxes or sawhorses in a dry, shady spot with good air circulation. Gently place the bulbs on the screen in a single layer. After a few days of curing, put the bulbs in a paper bag and place them in a dark, cool and well-ventilated location for storage.

Step 4. When you replant, reserve the largest bulbs for planting areas where you want the showiest displays. The smallest offsets will not flower in their first year and should be planted where you will know where they are, such as in a nursery row to grown bigger or as part of a naturalized planting where a few non-flowering bulbs won't be obvious. Like most other bulbs, daffodils grow best in well-drained soil in sun or light shade. I always add a bulb fertilizer, such as an organic 3-6-3 at this time as it gives the bulbs a gentle boost and will not burn any tender new roots. For spot planting, I dig the holes 8 inches deep and 8 inches apart. I place a tablespoon of the 3-6-3 in each hole and then insert the bulb and cover with soil. I do not like to put in a row of bulbs. Regardless of what bulb I am planting, I like to put them in "clumps" of color or variety. Not like little soldiers all in a row.

Step 5. Once planted, i.e. covered with soil and water them. Then I always cover the bulbs with 1 to 2 inches of mulch. Such as shredded bark leaf mold or compost. This helps conserve soil moisture and keeps down the weeds. I water the mulch this time. Chipmunks, moles and squirrels dislike daffodil bulbs, so they need no special protection. But those little rascals love crocuses and tulips.

Here is a hint for those of you, who like myself, love to bring flowers indoors. When cutting daffodils for you table, always choose ones that have not opened yet. They will open quickly in your vase and last a lot longer. Also, do not cut all the way down the stem and cut randomly through out your bed.

The following bulbs also can be divided:
Glory of the Snow (Chionodoxa): Divide after foliage dies; plant 3 inches deep; space 3 to 4 inches apart.

Grape hyacinths (Muscari): Divide summer to fall; plant 3 inches deep; space 3 to 4 inches apart.

Tulips (Tulipa): Divide after foliage dies; plant 6 to 8 inches deep; space 4 to 8 inches apart.

Squill (Scilla): Divide summer to fall; plant large species, such as S. peruviana, just below soil, others 3 to 4 inches deep; space 6 to 12 inches apart.

Always remember to buy the best bulbs you can afford, as they will reward you year after year, so in the long run, they are the best investment. Plus, try to find or start a local gardening club to trade your accumulating bulbs in the future years for things you do not have.

Monarch Visits Daffodil©

Chapter 3

Planting a Vegetable Garden

The trees are budding, the grass is growing, and you're thinking of all those wonderful garden plans you never got around to last year. This year, get a head start on the season with a few tips to help save time and avoid disappointment. And don't forget to involve the kids—this is one of the few times you can give them permission to play in the dirt!

Its time to start thinking about a vegetable garden! Don't ignore the plot of land you've always pictured as the ideal spot for a vegetable garden. Your dreams of a summer bounty full of vine-ripe tomatoes, fresh zucchini, crisp snap peas, and succulent green peppers can be realized. With a few simple guidelines for planning the perfect vegetable garden, you can enjoy a delicious harvest in summer and beyond! Don't make your first veggie garden too far from your house or water source. Don't make it too big. A small garden, planted correctly and maintained will give you plenty of produce.

Pick a Plot

The first step in successful gardening, and arguably the most important, is picking a spot. Make sure the area is large enough to accommodate the vegetables you want to plant, has good air circulation, and receives both sun and rainfall. Here are some tips to keep in mind when choosing your garden plot:
• Try not to plant too close to any large trees or hedges, as they can shade your garden and take the moisture and nutrients from the soil that your plants will need.
• With stakes and strings, mark off the areas where you will walk in your garden, and where you will plant your vegetables. You want to make sure you have enough room to move around without hurting your plants. It can also help to draw a rough diagram, and indicate where you want to plant certain vegetables.
• Allow enough growing space for your larger vegetables.
• Remember—it helps to provide stakes or trellises for vine plants.

Choosing Your Crop

Once you've selected your garden spot, you can start choosing the vegetables you want to grow. However, your local climate will determine *when* you can plant your seeds. You can find the information you need regarding when to plant on the back of your seed packets, and on many agricultural websites. Remember that some vegetables need to be started inside before they can be transplanted outdoors.

Cool versus Warm

Planting periods are determined by your choice of cool-season vegetables and warm-season vegetables. Cool-season vegetables are generally not harmed by light frost, but won't do well with extended periods of warm temperatures. They can usually be planted earlier in spring. These include cabbage, mustard, lettuce, celery, carrots, kale, onions, peas and spinach. Warm-season vegetables generally need a soil temperature of at least

50°F and can be killed by frost, so they need to be planted a little later in the season when there is no more danger of frost. These include cucumbers, sweet potatoes, peppers, tomatoes, squash and sweet corn.

If you are starting seedlings in vermiculite to get a jump on the season, great! But be sure to transplant them as soon as the second pair of true leaves form, or they'll starve.

Preparing the Soil

The soil must be the right temperature and consistency for planting. Soil that's too wet, too cold, or too warm (depending on your plants or seeds) won't produce a good crop. Before you plant, use a shovel to remove grass, weeds, and rocks from your garden plot. In addition, turn over the soil to break up any big lumps.

Get Your Vegetables in a Row

You can plant however you wish, but to get the best results, consider planting in rows or raised beds. Planting in rows is the more traditional method, and rows are easy to organize, maintain, and plant. Raised beds use space more efficiently, and you might not have to weed as much. However, raised beds take more initial time and money to prepare. Whichever route you take, make sure when you're planting to walk around the perimeter of your garden or in the pre-made walkways to avoid damaging your plants.

Hoe, Hoe, and more Hoe:

Your vegetable garden will need regular upkeep and removal of weeds to thrive. Weeds reduce the available nutrients, sunlight, soil, and space your plants need. There are many different ways to control weeds in your garden—including pulling, hoeing, and herbicides.

You can also try to stop the weeds before they start. A nice trick is to plant vegetables that suppress or shade weeds, which prevent further growth. You could try cucumbers, tomatoes, and squash. For this to work properly, it's best to make sure your suppression (or shading) vegetables have become established in the garden before weeds start to arrive.

Pests

Try to keep your garden organic. There are many ways to foil pests. Herbs are nature's insecticides. Basil planted near tomatoes, for example, will repel worms and flies. Nothing beats the fragrance of fresh herbs, and they're decorative as well. Some people like to use straw or mulch. However, mulches can keep the soil from warming up. So wait to apply organic mulches after plants are 3 to 4 inches tall and the soil is warm.

Watering

In addition to weeding, make sure your garden is properly watered. On average, plants need approximately one inch of water a week. If a plant starts to droop, revive it by watering right away.

There you have it—the simple basics you need to start the vegetable garden you always dreamed of having. With just a little time and effort, you can enjoy the fruits (and veggies!) of your labor.

Chapter 4

How to Know What Trees to Plant

At the end of every Louis L'Amour novel he asked his readers to plant one tree a year. His premise was that it only takes about 30 minutes to cut down a tree and it takes years for one to grow. He realized that millions of trees are cut each year and many are not being replaced. Today, the forestry industry replaces what it cuts, but developers and builders cut down many trees to build homes and rarely replace any. It is up to us to plant a tree.

Planting a tree is not a complex thing, but deciding what to plant and where to plant it is. Here are a few good hints for not only trees, but a few perennials, grasses when mentioned and perhaps a shrub or two.

If you have poor soil then consider planting Green Ash, Northern Bayberry, Black Eyed Susans, Dwarf Rose Hedge-Sandy, Black Locust, Osage Orange, Black Oak, Chestnut Oak, Eastern White Pine, Japanese Black Pine, Southwestern White Pine, Hybrid Poplar (for fast shade trees or for screens and windbreaks) and Virginia Pine. These trees will usually survive anywhere.

An Eastern White Pine is fast growing to about 100 ft. It is a five needled pine, with soft, light green-blue needles, about 4 inches long and it can tolerate dry, rocky soil. It grows well in normal moisture condition, but can even tolerate wet, swampy areas. It makes an excellent ornamental tree for naturalizing, windbreak or dense screen and can be easily restrained to a manageable height by pruning. For screen or Christmas trees just shear when new growth appears. This tree is easily controlled and is a good planting tree for small properties as well as field planting for those who want to grow trees for Christmas trees and timber. It grows well in zones 3 to 8.

If you live near a highway where your property will get salt spray from highway salt in the winter then consider planting Northern Bayberry, Dwarf Rose Edge-Sandy, Black Locust, Red Oak, White Oak, Japanese Black Pine or Colorado blue spruce.

When you think you might like to have a screen of Evergreens then any of these trees will easily do the trick: Canaan Fir, Canadian Hemlock, American Red Pine, Austrian Pine, Eastern White Pine, Black Hills Spruce, Colorado Blue Spruce, Norway Spruce, Serbian Spruce and White Spruce.

When you want to cultivate wildlife to your property then consider planting any of these trees: Northern Bayberry, Wild Black Cherry, White Flowering Dogwood, American Elder (Elderberry) American Mountainash, Black Mulberry, Chestnut Oak, Pin Oak, Red Oak, Sawtooth Oak, Northern Pecan, Persimmon, American Plum and Shadblow Serviceberry.

Nut trees take a long time to grow, but are worth the effort for the future and you might consider these trees: Butternut, Chinese Chestnut, American Hazelnut, Shagbark Hickory, Chestnut Oak, Pin Oak, Red Oak, Northern Pecan and Black Walnut.

When one has wet areas then consider these trees: European Alder, American Pyramidal Arborvitae, Buttonbush, silky Dogwood, Red Maple, Silver Maple, Pin Oak, Red Oak, Swamp White Oak, Eastern White Pine, American Sycamore, American Cranberrybush Viburnum, Bankers Dwarf Willow, Black Willow, Dappled Willow and Streamco Willow.

When you want brilliant fall color consider these trees: Burning Bush, Chinese Dogwood, Silky Dogwood, White Flowering Dogwood, Red Baron Grass, Black Gum, Washington Hawthorn, Red Maple, Sugar Maple, Red Oak, Shadblow Serviceberry, European Spindle Tree, Smooth Sumac, Stag horn Sumac and Witchhazel.

Don't forget to plant some shade trees. They will keep your home cool in the summer, give your kids a place to lie under and use their imagination, give you a place to put your hammock and get a half hour rest from your busy day. These shade trees are winners: Catalpa, Sweet Cherry, Black Gum, Thornless Honeylocust, Red Maple, Sugar Maple, Silver Maple, American Mountainash, Red Mulberry, Pin Oak, Red Oak, Scarlet Oak, White Oak and Hybrid Poplar for a fast growing shade tree.

When you have a place with a soil erosion problem, plant a tree! These work well: Northern Bayberry, Crownvetch, Black Chokeberry, Gray Dogwood, Siberian Dogwood, Silky Dogwood, Dwarf Rose Hedge-Sandy, Black Locust, Osage Orange, Bankers Dwarf Willow, Black Willow and Steamco Willow.

One of life's greatest pleasures is to see a flowering tree and these trees fill the bill: Catalpa, Mahaleb Cherry, Purpleleaf Sand Cherry, Sweet Cherry, Sargent Crabapple, Chinese Dogwood, White Flowering Dogwood, Cucumbertree Magnolia, Paulownia, American Plum, Eastern Redbud and Shadblow Serviceberry.

When you have a wooded area on your property and want to plant some shade tolerant trees then consider these trees: White Flowering Dogwood, Canadian Hemlock, English Ivy, Red Maple, Myrtle, Mountain Laurel, Pachysandra, Rosebay Rhododendron, Densiformis Low Spreading Yew and Wardii Spreading Yew.

A good Evergreen hedge can be formed using Elegantissima Pyramidal Arborvitae, Emerald Green Pyramidal Arborvitae, Green Giant Pyramidal Arborvitae, Threadleaf Arborvitae, Green Mountain Boxwood, Canadian Hemlock, Norway Spruce and Serbian Spruce.

Seeing deer out on your property is a pretty sight, but not to a gardener who is watching those critters eats their plants and gardening efforts. Here are some good deer resistant trees: Elegantissima Pyramidal Arborvitae, Dwarf Rose Hedge-Sandy, Blue Pacific Juniper, Blue Star Juniper, Saybrook Gold Juniper, Sea Green Juniper, Spartan Juniper,

Black Hills Spruce, Colorado Blue Spruce, Norway Spruce, Serbian Spruce and White Spruce.

As one can see as one reads along that many of these trees fit in many of the various categories. Also you will notice that occasionally I mentioned a perennial or a grass or shrub for a solution to a problem when I wrote the word trees. I know it and it is just a suggestion about what type of plant works in that area.

Also nowhere in this article did I mention the Bradford or Cleveland Pear tree which is a wonderful tree for lining your driveway. It gives you wonderful white flowers in the spring, beautifully green pear shaped trees in the summer and grand red leaves in the fall. It is a fast growing tree and very graceful.

I did not mention fruit trees, but they are great trees to plant also especially the dwarf fruit trees that will give you fruit within 4 to 5 years. We have an orchard that was planted by me and my late son Fred who unexpectedly passed away in August 2000. These trees are a living legacy to that dear boy and give me many memories of him and especially of the days we worked together planting those trees.

Just remember to read the directions on your trees when you plant them. Once you get them started they usually require no care. Also remember that as your tree grows taller it will grow wider, so make sure you allow for that.

In the fall, the leaves do exactly that on most trees, they "fall" to the ground. Leave them there. They are biodegradable and you will not see them in the following spring as they will have either blown away or disintegrated into the soil, thus building up top soil.

Dining Out on a Sno-Cone©

Chapter 5

How to Handle Little Garden Problems

I have a lot of clay around our home and in some place some sandy soil. However, I have found some plants that do well in the sandy soil. I planted drought-tolerant plants and watered them several times a week to get them established. Once they were well-rooted, they tolerated the dry growing conditions associated with sandy soil.

For sunny areas, try some of the following annuals: sunflower, zinnia, blanket flower, cosmos, cockscomb, gazania (treasure flower), portulaca, dusty miller, Dahlberg daisy, verbena and Mexican sunflower. And if you prefer perennials, try these sun-lovers: purple coneflower, black-eyed Susan, gayfeather, thyme, Artemisia, perennial sunflower, yucca, sedum, Russian sage, potentilla and ornamental grasses.
It's harder to find shade plants that will tolerate dry soil. But you can try perennials like deadnettle (Lamium), variegated archangel (Lamiastrum), lily-of-the-valley and coral bells.

Annuals such as periwinkle and the biennial Chinese forget-me-nots will also grow in dry, partially shaded locations.

Now that it is fall here is my "to do" list and it should be considered yours. This is one of my favorite times of the years. Besides the colors of the changing leaves I can look forward to a bountiful fall and a beautiful spring. This is the time I order spring-flowering bulbs for fall planting and I divide irises and other spring-flowering perennials. One can keep planting short-season vegetables like peas, lettuce, radishes and beats for a fall harvest. Of course one gets to harvest and preserve herbs for winter use and on the bird watching side this is the time to look for American goldfinches building nests as thistles produce down, their preferred nesting material and I get to try and watch as teenage birds begin to grow feathers that make them look more like their parents.

Do you have a hard time preventing weeds like I do? Try the following: mulch is a surface layer spread over the ground to conserve moisture, suppress weeds and maintain a good soil texture. Mulches may be organic, such as manure, compost, bark chips or cocoa shells, or non-organic, for example, stones, gravel or polythene sheeting.

Some people use weed killers and I basically stay away from them because we try to be completely organic at Home Farm Herbery. However, to save time and hard work weed killers are the answer to many people's problems. Just make sure you read the manufacturer's directions and warnings real well. Keep the weed killer off the plants you wish to keep. Dissolve and dilute the weed killer according to the manufacturer's directions and use a fine rose sprinkler head on a watering can you use only for weed killers. Don't apply on a windy day or it will drift or blow onto other plants. The best time to apply weed killer is when the weeds are leafy and actively growing which would be mid-spring to early summer. Remember, regardless of whatever the manufacturer touts many weeds do not die right off and need repeated treatments. Needless to say keep all chemicals away from your children and pets.

Most of us do not realize there are annual weeds and perennial weeds. An annual is a plant that normally completes its full cycle of growth, flowering and seeding in a single season, and then dies. Some annuals may be sown in autumn to flower the following spring. Annual weeds such as chickweed, groundsel, purple dead nettle, annual nettle, fat hen, opium poppy, hairy bittercress, annual meadow grass, speedwell and yellow oxalis have the same kind of growing cycle.

The aim of annual weeds is to grow and set is to grow and set seed as quickly as possible. They grow from seed on any recently cultivated soil and sometimes will grow on top of the newly placed mulch you put down to stop the weeds from growing. A vicious cycle isn't it? Seeds can survive for years in the soil, waiting for the perfect conditions to grow and then you wonder, "where the heck that one came from?" They germinate at lower temperatures than most garden plants, giving them a head start over their rivals! Once you recognize them at the seedling stage controlling annual weeds is relatively easy. Then you can keep from eliminating the vegetable or flower seedling that may be growing along side of them. Most hoe out easily or pull out when they get to be a pick able size. Just remember to eliminate the weed you must eliminate the root! Only put them on your compost heap if they do not have a seed head.

A perennial is any plant with an indefinite life span of more than two years. Some may be quite short-lived, whereas trees can easily survive for centuries. Likewise perennial weeds, such as dandelions, creeping thistle, brambles, dock, ragwort and stinging nettle have the same type of growing cycle. Yet they are more of a problem because they can live for several years. They survive winter by storing food in their roots. These roots make them harder to get rid of then annual weeds. Some are difficult to dig out and others spread underground so if you leave even the tiniest piece of root in the soil when you dig them out, be prepared to get a whole new plant.

The best way to control them is to dig out the whole plant as soon as you see them. So long as you do not let them produce leaves, they will use up their stored up food energy and eventually die. Never, never rotate soils with perennial weed infestation or you will have whole new colonies of weeds growing up in the new place. Always dig out every little bit as they grow and with twice the effort in order to control them. If you don't mind using chemicals, treat them with a weed killer containing glyphosate. Last but not least, never put perennial weed roots or seed-heads on to the compost heap.

One can try what is called root-proof barriers, which is a vertical barrier that will often stop rampant roots invading from next door. Just dig a 1 foot or 30 cm deep trench and bury the barrier. The best material to use is damp-proof course (DPC), available from all builders' supply store.

I keep getting asked a lot of questions about compost. One year I bought a Mantis Composter and I never did get the hang of it for the two years I played with it. I finally sold it on eBay and a guy came down Ohio to pick it up. Now composting is probably easy with one of those, but it was a real mystery for me. I guess I will stick to the old way of making a compost pile and turning it over every couple of days. When one talks about making a garden compost it usually means a garden compost made from waste materials rotted down in a compost heap, but it usually refers to the special soil or peat mixtures used for sowing and potting plants. There are two main kinds. Soil-less compost is made from peat or a substitute such as bark or coir. Soil-based composts are a mixture of sterilized soil, peat or an alternative, and sand. They all have added fertilizers.

A universal, soil-less compost is suitable for all normal sowing and potting needs, but there are different grades of soil-based compost. You can also buy special composts for rooting cuttings or for growing ericaceous (lime-hating) plants, orchids, and water plants.

Growing roses is really not a big problem and I have grown all kinds from the cheap $1.98 ones to the finer ones that cost a lot more. One of the lovelies climbing roses I have here in Kentucky is one I bought at a Publix's market in Vero Beach, FL. I brought it home from a vacation I was on in the winter of 1998 and proceeded to "kill" it off about 3 or 4 times over the next 2 years, but it is still growing strong as I write this in September of 2006 and produces lovely red roses year after year two or three times a season. I cannot even remember the name of it.

I have a hard time keeping the Rosie O'Donnell rose alive and have managed to have 3 of them over 3 seasons fail to make it through my zone 6 area. I do not think it is the zone, I think it is the soil even though the last one I planted in 2005 had a whole new area of dirt brought in just for it. The other one I love and have no luck with is Joseph's Coat.

One of the best one's I ever bought was an Albertine rose from The Antique Rose Emporium about 7 years ago for $14.95. It was a small root and now it looks the a huge stump with pink roses all up the side of our gift shop and across a wide rose arbor and all over half the roof of our Avalon Stained Glass School. It comes back and delivers the loveliest, most fragrant pink roses each June. All the others I bought from them that year have done well. But the nine I bought in 2005 from them at $17.95 each plus shipping have all died through this past winter which was a mild one here. I am heartily disappointed with them as they only warrant their roses for 90 days whereas Lowes' garden center, providing I keep the sales slip, will guarantee them for 12 months.

I try to find disease-resistant roses and in recent years I find in plant breeding they have created a number of roses that are resistant to black spot. In a bad year they will get it, but only a minor dose, thus the rest of the time they are usually trouble free. Here are a couple of my favorites.

 This one is Rosa Golden Showers. It is a yellow climbing rose with dark glossy green leaves. The height is about 6.5 ft with a spread of 7 feet. Just as there are many shrubby roses so there are many climbing roses, but this is one of the best. It is an upright climber and can be pruned to be a shrub. It produces a profusion of double flowers that are 10cm (4in) across.

 Another favorite is Rosa gallica, "Versicolor" or Rosa Mundi as many might know it by its common name. This red rose with a white stripe is a hardy shrub growing about 2.5 ft with a 3 ft spread with glossy green leaves. It is a lovely old and well-loved rose, neat and bushy. Particularly charming is the semi-double, slightly scented, flat flowers 5cm (2in) in diameter. This rose prefers full sun.

 *Rosa rugosa is a hedgehog rose that is a hardy shrub bearing* Purplish-red and white blossoms with glossy green leaves. This rose grows to 3ft to 6.6ft x 3ft to 6.6ft and is a dense, vigorous species rose with attractively wrinkled leaves. It bears a succession of flowers, 9cm (3.5in) in diameter. These are followed in late autumn by large tomato-shapes and colored fruit (hips.)

 Rosa "Iceberg" is another favorite shrub rose with a pure white flower and glossy green leaves. It is a good compact plant about 2.5 ft by 2.1 ft. This bush rose produces many sprays of graceful double, cupped-shaped flowers up to 7cm (3in) in diameter that look fantastic against the dark leaves. It also responds well to heavy pruning.

I hope this little chapter will help you keep abreast of the many challenges that any gardener faces. In the event I can help you with anything else just send an email to askarlene@scrtrc.com and I will try my best to help you.

Monarch Visits Echinacea©

Chapter 6

How to Grow Columbines

 Columbines are often called Grannies Bonnets or Wild Columbine, but their Latin name is Aquilegia Vulgaris and they have been around since they were grown in England since 1600. When they are planted in the correct part of your garden they will prove to be a very hardy, perennial, with clump-forming plants that have lovely grey/green foliage and grow to 36 inches.

The flowers can be pink or purplish/blue color and they look good when planted with shrubs or in borders with irises or poppies. I like to use them where I plant tulips for as the tulips die back the aquilegias grow up to help cover the fading leaves.

Columbines like moist soil but it has to be well drained. They do best in partial shade but will grow readily in full sun if you have dug in plenty of well rotted compost and as long as you remember to water them regularly for they do not like their roots to dry out and they are not fussy as to the type of soil it can be chalky or acidic.

All Columbine/Aquilegias self seed *very easily* so nip the seed heads off before they go brown, if you do not want this to happen and their flower heads can be removed to extend their flowering period. Should they develop mildew through lack of water then cut back to the ground and the plant will grow again in the same place.

Keep the varieties apart from one another if you want them to stay true, as they readily hybridize amongst themselves! Columbine/Aquilegias can be divided in autumn and winter or you can sow seed in spring or autumn. If you like antique or old varieties then you should consider the variety named *Nora Barlow* which is sometimes called the Rose Columbine and dates from the seventh century.

It is an English garden favorite and it can be an American garden favorite with lovely reddish/pink and pale green blooms, like little pom-poms and has a scent of hay. It is very good as a cut flower and the Victorians who were very fond of them, used to grow them amongst shorter perennials beside paths where they could clearly be appreciated.

In the past it is noted that Columbines were used to treat sore throats and as an antiseptic. Today all parts are considered **poisonous** and therefore should not be eaten.

Chapter 7

Some Thoughts about Flowers
(This chapter runs amok with a myriad of information on growing, drying and arranging flowers)

When words escape, flowers speak. While they may not last as long as diamonds, flowers are forever. We associate flower with the special times of our lives. Birthdays, marriages, farewells…No occasion goes without the fragrance of flowers.

When we wish to convey passion, respect, congratulations, or apology to the people most precious to us, only flowers will do.

Flower- The Perfect gifts

Flowers are the perfect gifts for any occasion, especially for those close to us.
Flowers always bring on a smile and brighten up our day. Sending flowers to someone always make a person feel special. Many people described the flowers in different ways.

John Ruskin had associated the kindness of a person to the flower as

> *"Kind hearts are the garden,*
> *Kind thoughts are the root*
> *Kind words are the blossoms,*
> *Kind deeds are the fruit."*

In his poem **"The Daffodils"**, the great poet William Wordsworth writes about the attraction the sight of a garden of golden **daffodil flower** holds and the effect the beauty of the flowers has on a person.

> *"I wandered lonely as a cloud*
> *That floats on high o'er vales and hills,*
> *When all at once I saw a crowd,*
> *A host, of golden daffodils;*
> *Beside the lake beneath the trees,*
> *Fluttering and dancing in the breeze."*

He sees the daffodil flower as a representation of everything sprightly and jovial. The sight of the dancing daffodil leaves such an imprint of cheer and glee on his mind that whenever he sits gloomy, he finds inspiration and joy from the memories of the daffodils. The smile of the daffodil almost becomes an inner voice which drives away his loneliness.

Planting Daffodil Flowers
Glynis gave me some daffodil bulbs for my birthday and she planted them down by the mail box at the end of the driveway. As of this writing they have not come up yet. I firmly believe that Daffodils, like tulips and hyacinths should be planted in the fall.

Daffodils are perhaps the world most popular choice among the bulbs to be planted in the gardens.

The best characteristics of Daffodils are that they are suitable for being planted in any landscape. They can be lined up beside your driveway or walkway, you can plant daffodils flowers around deciduous trees or plant them independently in clusters in gardens or place them in pots at your doorstep. Wherever you plant the daffodils, they will bring color and beauty to your home.

The attraction of the daffodil flowers lies in their variety of colors. Daffodils come in every wide range of colors and sizes. Daffodils are also one of the permanently flowering plants. The daffodils grow every year. In fact, their growth increases every year. Daffodils flowers can also withstand hot summers and cold winters.

So, it is easy see why planting daffodil flowers can be a very attractive addition to your garden.

Ideal time for planting Daffodil flowers
Thanksgiving Day is past. The soil temperature will be cool now. This is perhaps the best time for plating daffodil flowers.

Origins of Daffodil flowers
Daffodil flowers have been believed to have their origins in Asia and Southern Europe. The Daffodils are commonly known as the Trumpet flowers. This is because of the common variety of daffodil flowers which has a long cup that is surrounded by six long petals, giving it the resemblance to a trumpet

Daffodil flowers are available in different varieties; in fact there have been about 25,000 different daffodil flower types.

Now let us learn a few tips for planting daffodil flowers:
The first thing we have to do while planting daffodil flowers is of course to choose the daffodil bulbs you want to plant.

Planting daffodil flowers:
Choosing daffodil flowers

Daffodil bulbs can be bought at any nursery or garden centers. To purchase more unusual varieties, look for catalogs that specialize in bulbs, particularly Dutch bulb catalogs. Daffodil flowers are separated into different sizes based on their noses and tips. The daffodil bulbs are designated as DNI or DNII. These names indicate whether each daffodil bulb will be producing one flower or two flowers.
Bulbs are sized by their noses or tips. Look for the designations DN I or DN II when purchasing. This indicates that each bulb will produce one or two flowers.

When choosing bulbs, remember that a naturalizing group will bloom intermittently over a long period of time. If you choose to go with one or two varieties, you will have most of your blooms at the same time.

Planting daffodil flowers: Soil Requirements

Soil which is not too dry is the best suitable soil for planting daffodils.
The soil for planting the daffodils should be loose. Plant the daffodils about 5 to 8 inches deep in the soil. The exact depth to which the daffodil flowers will be planted depends upon the size of the bulb size. The larger bulbs will be planted deeper than the smaller bulbs. Leave a space of about 2 to 6 inches between each bulb.

Planting daffodil flowers: Use of fertilizers

Adding fertilizers to daffodil flower plants is not an absolutely necessary. But adding fertilizers can be good for the development of the daffodil flowers.

Planting daffodil flowers: Watering Daffodil plants

Watering daffodil flowers is very important. The daffodil flowers need moisture continuously. Daffodil flowers cannot grow in dry conditions. So keep watering the daffodil flowers regularly to keep them moist and fresh.
When displaying daffodils as cut flowers, be aware that daffodils and tulips do not mix well in the same vase. The sap from the daffodils will kill the tulips. To make them compatible, place the daffodils in a separate vase for 24 hours before mixing with tulips. If you want the daffodil flowers to be healthy and continue flowering for coming years, fertilize after blooming is over. After that, keep adding fertilizers every two weeks.
Don't ever cut the foliage before it dies back. The daffodil bulbs use the nutrients from the foliage to continue blooming every year.

Thanksgiving Decoration Tips

Thanksgiving is one occasion which brings as much joy and festivities as Christmas.

Thanksgiving sees decorations and celebrations all around. People organize get together for complete families and enjoy the Thanksgiving dinner with family and friends.
Everybody takes time to decorate their homes for Thanksgiving. A beautiful centerpiece for the dining table, flower bouquets and flower vases with fragrant flowers, all play a part in making your home pleasant and inviting for your guests.

Here are some Thanksgiving decoration tips to complete your Thanksgiving decorations in smaller budgets. Using flowers from your garden and simple decorative pieces from your own home may make your Thanksgiving decoration cheaper and also give you the satisfaction of creating things and making the decorations on your own.

Thanksgiving decoration tips

Thanksgiving decoration tip 1: Follow a color scheme. The autumn flavor is colors like bright yellow and red. Make these colors your choice while you are buying ribbons and other fabrics for bouquets and other decorations.

Thanksgiving decoration tip 2: Gather the flowers. If you don't want to spend much on the flowers or if you have a garden with useful flower blooms, take time to collect flowers and twigs. Go outdoors and choose all the flowers, sticks and branches that may be useful for your decorations.

Thanksgiving decoration tip 3: Centerpiece is the main attraction.
Without a doubt the centerpiece will be the main catcher of all your Thanksgiving decorations. Use the flower blooms and the branches that you collected to make an attractive centerpiece for your table.

First select an attractively shaped branch. Glue your leaves and braches to this main branch. Make sure you follow the basic shape of the centerpiece that you intend to create. The generally used Thanksgiving decoration centerpieces will be either round or cone shape. Keep in mind the shape that you want to create.

Fill in greens in the centerpiece to draw attention to the colors of the flowers used and also to fill in the centerpiece without leaving any gaps.

Thanksgiving decoration tip 4: Accessories for your Centerpiece. Once the centerpiece is completed, you can keep it on the table. Place some attractive Indian corn and gourds from a local grocery store next to the centerpiece on the table.

Thanksgiving decoration tip 5: Use lots of candles. Candles have a very inviting luster that lights up the room. Make use of the warmth of the candles to illuminate your house and add attraction to your decorations. Select candles of different sizes and shapes. Candles displayed in the right corners can provide an ambient atmosphere in the room.

Follow the above Thanksgiving decoration tips to add your personal touch to your home decorations this Thanksgiving. Just remember – it takes just a bit of interest, lots of patience and a bit of imagination; make the time – You will be pleasantly surprised by the results.

ROSE--The Queen of flowers

The rose is the oldest domesticated flower known; fossilized imprints found in Florissant, Colorado, indicate that roses existed around 40 million years ago. Throughout out history roses have been symbols of love beauty, war and politics. Roses inspire passion even in disagreement. Modern roses come in all sizes, shapes and colors.

Glynis' Roses©

Stem lengths and blooming habits also differ for each variety. Rose varieties can be vastly different in both appearance and performance. They will open at different rates and in different ways.

Some will open widely (such as Konfetti, Orange Unique and Black Magic) while others will just unfurl (such as Ilio, Gypsy Curiosa and Nicole).

Roses of different colors represent different emotions.
Red rose: Love; I love you
Pink rose: Perfect happiness
Deep pink rose: Thank you
Light pink rose: Admiration
Dark crimson rose: Mourning
White rose: Innocence and purity
White with red roses: Unity
Yellow rose: Friendship

Even the way the Roses are presented symbolize different moods and carry different messages.
Bouquet of roses in full bloom: Gratitude
Garland or crown of roses: Beware of virtue; reward of merit; crown, symbol of superior merit
Single full bloom: I love you
Tea rose: I'll remember always
Thornless Rose: Love at first sight
Dried white rose: Death is preferable to loss of virtue
Withered white rose: Transient impression; fleeting beauty; you made no impression

Rose leaf : You may hope
Rose bud: Beauty and youth; a heart innocent of love
Red rosebud: Pure and lovely
White rosebud: Girlhood
Damask rose: Brilliant complexion
Cabbage rose: Ambassador of love
Christmas rose: Tranquilize my anxiety; anxiety

Lilac Flower

Lilac flower welcome the spring with their enchanting fragrance. Lilac flowers are known for their charm and their fragrance. Initially, the lilac flower were seen in only a few colors- mostly purple and white but there are many varieties, colors and shapes of lilac flower available now.

Lilac flower: Fragrance

The most obvious feature of a lilac flower is its fragrance. Different varieties of lilac flower show various degrees of fragrance- ranging from slightly sweet to pungent. White lilac flower is known to give out the best fragrance.

Lilac flower: Overview

Lilac flower belongs to genus Syringa. The lilac flower is native to Asia. The common lilac flower belongs to species S.Vulgaris. All the lilac flowers of syringa species are known for their attractive fragrance. And among all lilac flowers, the most fragrant is the S.pubescens. This lilac flower is native of China and gives a very pleasant, sweet scent.

Lilac flower: Shrubs and trees.

The lilac flower grows on shrubs. Sometimes these shrubs can become very large growing to a considerable size. On the other hand, we can also actually find some lilac flower trees. These lilac flower trees can grow to a size of a mango tree . They provide good shade

Lilac flower: Flowering

The lilac flower trees give flowers very late compared to other common lilac plants. They usually flower about one week to 10 days later after the early lilac flowers bloom. But the late lilac flower blooms have a distinctive smell and these are mostly hybrid plants

Growing lilac flower plants

Growing lilac flower plants is very easy. The lilac flower doesn't need a lot of food or a lot of care. So it is easy to grow lilac flower and take care of them. Lilacs need good sun, and should be planted in good garden soil with a slightly alkaline nature. Lilac flower grows best in cold climate.

LILAC--In winters

It is a shrub that does best where winters are cold but there are varieties (most called Descanso hybrids) for mild-winter climate also and many more.

Growing and Caring Azalea plants

Spring brings with it the beautiful blooms of Azalea plants. Azalea plants are beautiful semi evergreen shrubs. They are a kind of Rhododendron flowers and belong to the family Ericaceae.

Called "the royalty of the garden", Azalea plants are found in almost every area except Africa and South America. They are widely seen in Southeastern Asia, North America and Southern Europe. A distinctive feature of Azalea plants are large clusters of pink, red, orange, yellow, purple, or white flowers. Azaleas form flower buds in late summer and autumn, and bloom in the spring. Gentle forcing will produce flowers in the house during the winter and very early spring. Azalea plants are best suited for use in an informal garden that has partial shade.

Unlike non-azalea rhododendrons which have flowers in trusses- which are groups of many flowers, Azalea plants have single flowers rather than trusses.
Many hybrid azalea plants have been created and about 10000 different species have been created so far. Plant enthusiasts continue to grow new azalea plant varieties.

AZALEA--The blooms
Flowering indoor azaleas bloom in a variety of colors such as white, pink, lavender, and coral. Azaleas prefer bright filtered light and even moisture. Indoor azaleas are kept as foliage plants after blooming because they are not hardy but can be placed outdoors for the summer and into the cool fall days. Azaleas should then be brought indoors and kept cool until it blooms again.

Pink Azalea plant
Pink azalea plant is very appealing with beautiful blooms and nice fragrance. Pink azalea presents delicate individual blooms. Azalea plants show terminal blooms-that is one flower per flower stem. There are many stems and when they flower, they appear as bunches of colorful specks.

Growing Azalea plants

Planting Azalea flowers plants

Azaleas are grown from seed and propagated by stem cuttings. Though Azalea flowers grow best in spring, Azalea flowers can be grown at any time of the year. Fall is however the best time to plant new azalea flowers plants.

Purchasing Azalea plants

While buying an Azalea plant, the size of the plant is not important. You can also buy either an azalea plant which is potted or a stem wrap.

Consider however, the possible final size of the flowers and the resistance and cold bearing capacity of the plant. These details will be given at the nurseries.
Azalea plants grow to small heights, sometimes reaching a maximum of only two feet. Some azalea plants can on the other hand grow to heights of twelve feet. Your choice should depend on your requirement and the layout of your garden.

You can also balance the blooming of the flowers by a bit of planning certain plants which bloom early in the season and some which bloom later. This will keep up a presence of azalea flowers blooms throughout the season.

Azalea plant requirements

Azalea plants need to be grown in acid soil, with a pH of around 5.0 to 6.5 . Materials that make soils more acid are ferrous sulfate or copperas, iron chelate, and finely ground dusting sulfur. Adding liberal amounts of peat moss and decaying oak leaves also tends to make the soil more acid.

Azalea plants must be planted in areas receiving direct sunlight in the mornings for a few hours.

The Azalea plants should be in shade during the hottest part of the day.

Planting Azalea flower plants

To plant the azalea root ball, you should dig a whole which is double its size and goes about 1-11/2 times deeper. Mix compost and peat moss into the soil.

Loosen up the roots of the azalea plant when you are removing it from the plant and planting in the ground. This will make them adjust better to the new soil.

Add a small amount of rhododendron food into the hole.

Now fill up the hole neatly and water it very thoroughly.

Maintain the azalea plants very carefully.

Remember that the buds for the next year's blooms will be formed now. You need to remove the faded and dried blooms to facilitate budding.

Azalea plants grow slowly and rarely need pruning. However, to maintain them at a certain size or to increase the density of their growth, azaleas may be pruned immediately after they've completed flowering, just as the new growth is being produced. These shrubs bloom each spring on the previous season's growth, having formed buds by summer's end, so don't prune them after early summer lest you sacrifice next year's flowers.

Ranunculus Flowers

I have yet to plant a Ranunculus, but I know a little about them.

Ranunculus pronounced as ran-UN-kew-lus is a latin word meaning "little frog". Ranunculus flowers have their origins in the Middle East; hence they are called as Turban Buttercup. The Ranunculus has tuberous roots and hollow stems.

In the language of Flowers Ranunculus flowers have the meaning of "you are rich in attractions".

Ranunculus--The Spring flowers are bright, rounded flowers atop dense green parsley-like foliage. A great plant for spring color with shades of red, purple, yellow, white, pink, and orange typically not kept as a houseplant, but can be used outdoors in the spring and summer.

Ranunculus flowers Colors
Ranunculus flowers are seen in winter and spring. Ranunculus flowers are found in many different attractive colors like the yellow, white, red and pink. You can even find copper Ranunculus flowers and the and also Ranunculus flowers with dark and yellow circles. Ranunculus flowers are brilliantly colored and are very attractive and special. The Ranunculus flowers are mostly in multiple layers with very thin petals. Ranunculus flowers can also be very long-lasting cut flowers. Ranunculus bulbs are also available widely and especially in mild-winter climates. Ranunculus flowers last up to six weeks. Ranunculus flowers are mostly fully double, 3-6 inches. The Bloomingdale variety however has a very short stem and flowers as double flowers.

Ranunculus Flowers care:

Tips: Remove all foliage, re-cut stems and change water regularly. The stems are inclined to buckle. If you don't want them curvy, insert a flower wire to keep them upright.

Tips for growing Ranunculus flowers

Step 1: Choosing Ranunculus tubers
Ranunculus tubers can be very dry and hard when you are choosing them in a store, but they can get very softened and plump by absorbing moisture. There is no need to soak them in water before planting. The moisture they absorb themselves is mostly enough. More water can make them like a much and useless for planting.

Step 2: Choose a location

For planting the Ranunculus flowers, the location should be very sunny and the soil should be well drained. The cool soil of fall and early spring offers some protection from rotting, but soil that is never soggy gives extra insurance.

Step 3: Planting Ranunculus flowers
The Ranunculus tubers should be planted with their claws pointing end down. Space them 8 to 12 inches apart.

Ranunculus flowers as cut flowers
Ranunculus flowers can last up to 7 days after being cut, This makes them a good cut flower. Ranunculus flowers are also comparatively very inexpensive.
Ranunculus flowers are to be cut when they first show color in the early mornings. The moisture they absorb at nights gives them their best possible color and look in the early hours.

Arranging Flowers

A nice flower arrangement is a pleasure to watch and brightens up the whole room.

Arranging flowers in a lovely arrangement in the entrance hall or as a centerpiece for the dining room. Everyone loves a nicely arranged flower vase which spreads fragrance all around arranging flowers can be a very simple task but give immense creative satisfaction.

Gladiolas©

Arranging orchid flowers is easier than arranging flowers of any other type. Because, when simply placed in the vase, the orchids arch down and fill the complete space the vase covers. They fall in a nice shapely arrangement by themselves.

Steps for arranging flowers
- For arranging flowers in a loose arrangement, you can just clip the ends of the stems .
- Catch all flowers in a hand and clip out the extra ends .making a nice overall shape.
- Place the bunch in the vase and adjust the flowers to fill the vase on completely stretch them further around to.
- You can trim the flowers regularly to keep the flowers fresh for longer time.

Arranging flowers: Growing hobby

Arranging flowers and making flower bouquets is becoming a favorite hobby for many people –of all ages. Many people are opting for arranging flowers themselves for presenting to their loved ones on birthdays, anniversaries and other different occasions. This way, along with the lovely message that flowers alone can convey, flower arrangements add a personal creative touch to the gift.

Benefits of arranging flowers
Arranging flowers can be a very relaxing activity and can bring forth your creative talent and can be lots of fun. You can save money by making your own arrangements for gifting friends. Also arranging flowers can be very economical if you have habit of giving out flower arrangements for a large group of friends on many occasions to say nothing that it can be a very pleasant hobby and a great stress reliever.

Tips for arranging flowers
Explained below are some simple tips for arranging flowers to make the perfect flower arrangement.
Arranging Flowers Tip 1: Maintain Balance
For arranging flowers in a symmetric manner, imagine a vertical line in the center. Place similar flowers on both sides of this line at same angle. Place flowers with longer stems

nearer to this line.

Arranging Flowers Tip 2: Choose nice Colors

Don't choose all dark or all light flowers .Try to select a good combination of dark and light colored flowers. But while arranging flowers, keep in mind not to place all dark flowers together. Don't ever place the dark flowers on the top since they will appear darker in light.

Arranging Flowers Tip 3: Size of the Flower arrangement

The size of the flower arrangement should be around one and half times the size of the container.

Arranging Flowers Tip 4: Keep in cool place

Before arranging flowers in to the vase, keep them in cool place. You can cut the tips of the stems and place them in lukewarm water and store them in cool place.

Arranging Flowers Tip 5: Add Lemon –lime soda

Adding a quarter of lemon-lime soda to three-quarters of water will keep the flowers fresh for longer periods.

Victorian Flowers
"Nothing sends a message like flowers. Flowers speak a language of their own"
.

When one hears the word "Victorian," flowers immediately come to mind. Flowers adorned everything Victorian, from wallpapers to young girl's samplers. Their beauty and colors were used in Victorian times to communicate feelings between friends, lovers and acquaintances. They were sent in bouquets, given singly, and printed on postcards. So it isn't surprising to know that the Victorians created a effective mode of communication using their beloved flowers.

Victorian flowers: Floriography (the language of flowers)
Victorian women elaborated on Floriography i. e. assigning meanings to flowers. Flowers afforded the Victorian women a silent language. They used the Victorian flowers to communicate any sentiments that the society of those times would not normally allow.

This communication using flowers became very popular among lovers. Even today this practice is followed. Not only flowers but also anything like a handkerchief carrying the smell of the particular plant would convey the same message.
Of course, more than one type of flower may be used to convey one's message, just as one flower can have many meanings depending upon color and size.

Messages of Victorian flowers

Single flowers could convey feelings just as strongly as an arrangement. Presenting these flowers to the receiver in the upright position is a friendly gesture and upside down had the opposite meaning.

The message didn't have to be conveyed through a live flower, necessarily. Either card such as decorated with the right flowers could speak volumes. A personal gift such as a floral embroidered hanky revealed feelings also.

Victorian flowers: Language
Even Queen Victoria believed in the language of Victorian flowers. So she had Myrtle (a kind of flower) in her bridal bouquet which symbolizes love and marriage. She later planted it. So even to this day, at every royal wedding in England, a piece of her myrtle is either tucked into the bride's bouquet, or is added to one of the floral arrangements at the wedding breakfast.

Lavender flowers
Lavender flowers add beauty to your garden by their variety of colors and their rich foliage. Lavender colors are found in a wide range of colors - from the pure white color to the bright purples.

The Lavender leaves are also very colorful and add to the attraction of the lavender flowers. Apart from the beauty of the blooms, lavender flowers are also useful in many other ways. Dried lavender flowers are used potpourri to oil, in preparation of aromatherapy products, colognes, lotions and soaps. Lavender wands are also very popular in use.

The Lavender Fields©

LAVENDER flowers --For the fragrance
Lavender flowers are considered to be one of the most versatile flowers in the world. Not only are the lavender flowers beautifully grown in the garden with its gray-green foliage and sweet smelling flowers, it is sought-after for hundreds of other uses.

Lavender flowers is antibacterial, anticonvulsive, antidepressant, anti-inflammatory, analgesic, antispasmodic, antitoxic, antiviral, anticoagulant, carminative, cordial, deodorant, decongestant, diuretic, hypotensive, insecticidal, parasiticidal, restorative, sedative, tonic, vermifugal, and vulnerary.

Lavender flowers work well in the treatment of acne, eczema, dermatitis, fungus, burns and wounds. Research shows that lavender is beneficial for the treatment of indigestion, hypoglycemia, hypertension, arteriosclerosis, kidney stones and anemia. It is non-toxic, non-irritant and non-sensitizing.

Besides its countless medicinal properties, lavender has many uses around the home, in the car and at the office. Used alone or blended together with other flowers, leaves, and pods, lavender potpourri is delightful to perfume an entire room. Hence lavenders are very useful.

Lavender flowers: Marital Bliss
Many legendary stories associate lavender flowers with marital bliss and harmony among a married couple. It is believed that the couple who place *lavender flowers* on their bed will never quarrel. In fact, using *lavender flowers* in decorating rooms can be seen in many traditions.

Lavender flowers are available in different varieties -some of which are the Spanish lavender (Lavandula stoechas) and French lavender (L. dentata).All these varieties of *lavender flowers* were used as herbs in Roman baths.

Some *lavender flowers* come with different unusual flower heads. Some lavender flowers are identified through their flower heads and sizes, while some other lavender flowers are identified, some other *lavender flowers* standout in the garden among other flowers for their attractive, while others are garden standouts for the color and shape of their foliage

Some other lavender flowers
Some other lavender flowers varieties are the 'Silver Frost', 'Ana Luisa', 'Richard Gray', and 'Sawyers'

Lavender flowers: As dry flowers

Lavender flowers are also used a lot as dry flowers also. Dark purple flowers are mostly used as dry flowers. For the use as dry flowers, dark *lavender flowers* are preferred. Many people find that the darker the lavenders, the more attractive they will are.
Lavender flowers plants which are smaller-growing, mound-forming make great edging plants. The English lavender falls under this category.
Lavender flowers which grow tall make fine hedging plants. Tall lavender plants have larger foliage and have longer flower stalks, hence they can catch more wind and provide movement in the garden.
Lavender flowers plants like sun and well-draining soil and grow best in such soil. The *lavender flowers* where the plant is nourished well and planted in well aired soil bloom in bright colors and stays longer.
Different Types of flowers
The beauty of the flowers lies in their softness, their pleasant fragrance and their different colors. Many flowers come in different colors , some of which are found commonly but

some colors are rare and this rarity add a which adds their beauty and makes them even more exotic.

Types of flowers for occasions
There are many flowers which have become so much a part of life by being used for so many occasions that it is difficult to remember the specific emotion they represent. But still even the colors of flowers and the different ways of presenting a bouquet can mean different messages.

Different uses of different types of flowers
Going to some of the interesting facts about flowers, where does the fragrance of flowers come from?

Fragrance in flowers is nature's way of encouraging pollination. Just as fragrance draw people to take a deeper breath it lures insects to blossoms hidden by leaves and other plants. Some flowers are fragrant only at night times and attract only night flying pollinators while others are more fragrant during the day times. The fragrance comes from essential oils called attars that vaporize easily and infuse the air with their scents. They are present in different combinations in different in different flowers.
Apart from conveying messages, giving out fragrance, flowers are of high medicinal value and are used in different medicines.

The Japanese people have great respect towards flowers because they form a part of their art. Inside their homes many Japanese have an alcove or special place that is decorated with flowers and plants to show the changing of the seasons. Japanese people often make field trips (like "pilgrimages") to see the flowers and trees in different seasons.

Amaryllis Flowers

Amaryllis flowers History
Amaryllis flowers history is very fascinating. Presently the **amaryllis flowers** are usually associated with Holland mostly but the *amaryllis flowers* have not originated in that place.

Around 1828, a young doctor Uduard Frederich Poepping was hunting for plants in Chile. In this expedition, he spotted very vibrant blooms on a Chilean mountain.

Beauty of Amaryllis flowers
He was amused by their beauty and is said to have shouted with joy at the spectacular sight of the beautiful amaryllis flowers. The name amaryllis flowers are based on the name of Greek Mythology- Amaryllis is the name of a Greek Shepherdess. The amaryllis flowers later reached Europe where they were hybridized. The hybridizers from Holland experimented with the different varieties of the Amaryllis flowers and made the large-flowered amaryllis flowers that can be seen today.

Other names of amaryllis flowers

Amaryllis flowers are also called as the flowering bulb Hippeastrum. Modern hybrids of Amaryllis flowers are called Giant Amaryllis flowers or the Royal Dutch amaryllis flowers.

Colors of Amaryllis flowers

Amaryllis flowers are noted for their flamboyance and the delightful colors. The amaryllis flowers are known for their bright colors and their big flowers. Now, almost two centuries later, their flamboyant, robust flowers continue to delight. They are sold at nurseries and garden centers as indoor flowering plants. Amaryllis is perfect for adding colorful punch to buffet tables, sophisticated cocktail parties or traditional family gatherings.

Amaryllis flowers for decorations
Apart from the holiday seasons when amaryllis flowers are in much use for decorations in parties and other occasions, amaryllis flowers can be enjoyed all the year long. The amaryllis flowers varieties flower from spring through winter in places such as the San Diego. Amaryllis flowers become very soft and tender in the cold climates.

Growing Amaryllis flowers
Growing amaryllis flowers is very easy. Planting and growing amaryllis flowers is so easy that it can be said that any person who cannot grow amaryllis flowers may very well quit the idea of gardening. "They want to grow and flower, even without water or sun light," Threadgill says. "If a person can't grow an amaryllis, then it's better to take up bowling or some other hobby than gardening."

Amaryllis flowers: Climate
In a moderately cool climate, amaryllis bulbs stay fresh and healthy for nearly an year. In warmer temperatures, the amaryllis flowers flower in about two to four weeks. The amaryllis flowers don't grow very well only in one month of the year- August.

Amaryllis flowers as Holiday gifts
Amaryllis flowers are associated mostly with fall through winter. Amaryllis flowers are a very popular in the holiday season as gifts for friends and for decorations. The actual time for amaryllis flowers to bloom is in the months of May and June. But the amaryllis flowers are dug from the ground and chilled for blooming in the months of December. Amaryllis flowers can grow in December provided they have been chilled for many months. But this is true for only some varieties of the amaryllis flowers. Some of such varieties are the South African bulbs. When the bulbs are dug out and planted in pots, the amaryllis flowers appear in about one month. The South African bulbs are sold as Christmas amaryllis.

Amaryllis flowers: Varieties
With growing popularity, an amaryllis flower is being grown in different areas and indifferent colors. The amaryllis flowers are now not restricted to a few colors such as the

white, orange, red, and pink. The amaryllis flowers are now grown in different colors and different sizes. The new amaryllis flowers are even available as double colored flowers and bloom in bold colors, pastels and bicolor.

Amaryllis flowers: Categories
Amaryllis flowers are separated into five main categories. The five categories are : Large flowered, small flowered, trumpets, double-flowered and cybister.

Large flowered amaryllis flowers: Large-flowered are the most popular and widely grown. The large flowered amaryllis flowers are about 8 to 10 inches in diameter. The stems of these large amaryllis flowers also grow to about 2 feet tall. The large flowered amaryllis flowers are available in a range of colors, bicolor or striped.

Small-flowered amaryllis flowers: Small-flowered amaryllis flowers are called miniature amaryllis flowers produce flowers which are up to 3 to 5 inches in diameter on stems of up to 12 to 15 inches. The amaryllis flowers bulbs of this variety are often a little smaller.

Trumpet Amaryllis flowers: Trumpet amaryllis flowers are named so because of the shape of the flowers. These amaryllis flowers resemble lilies. These flowers are lightly scented.

Double flowered Amaryllis flowers: Double-flowered amaryllis flowers refer to the increased number of petals on each flower head. The trumpet amaryllis is available in pure red, pure white, or with red or blush pink edges and stripes.

Cybister amaryllis flowers: Cybister amaryllis flowers are perhaps the most unusual type of amaryllis flowers. This variety was developed by a San Diego-area plant breeder, the late Fred Meyer. The cybister amaryllis has been derived from the Brazilian species . These hybrids have long, narrow petals with finely striped splashes of green or burgundy.

Amaryllis flowers: Price range
Large amaryllis bulbs (30-32 cm.) can range in price from $8.95 to $20; miniature, cybister and trumpet amaryllis are about $10 to $12.

Growing Amaryllis flowers
As we have mentioned earlier, growing amaryllis flowers is very easy. Here is the procedure for planting amaryllis flowers. To place the amaryllis flowers, choose a container only slightly larger than the bulb. Place the bulb in the container and add potting soil making sure that the top of the bulb, where it tapers upward, is above soil level. Water thoroughly, and then keep soil moist but not soggy until growth begins. Place container in sunny location. If there isn't enough light, the stalk may grow excessively. When flowers appear, move to a place with less light to preserve flower color and length of bloom. Some large-flowered varieties grow so tall that they may require staking. You can also grow several bulbs together in a larger, but not deeper container. Miniature amaryllis is especially showy in this type of display.

After blooming, remove spent stalks several inches above the bulb top. Return pot to a sunny location to promote healthy leaves, which help supply food for next year's flowers.

If you want to keep them in pots, keep watering and fertilize monthly with a water-soluble houseplant fertilizer. Some varieties are evergreen; others lose their leaves. Plants ultimately will revert to their normal bloom period of May and June.

Amaryllis flowers also can be planted in a landscape here. For coastal gardens, select a sunny location. Inland, they do better with afternoon shade, which keeps flowers from fading.

National Flowers
National flowers of different countries
National flowers are representation symbols of the respective countries.

Many nations have chosen flowers as national symbols. Some countries automatically give a picture of a flower which is mostly found in or other wise strongly associated with the country. This flower can be automatically treated as the national flower of that country.

Here is a list of some of the national flowers.

Some nations have adopted a particular flower as the national flower
owing to their history and tradition while some nations have chosen their national flowers according to conscious thought.

For whatever the reason, flowers chosen as the national flowers have become a national logo.

Country	National Flower
Australia	Golden Wattle
Canada	Maple Leaf
China	Narcissus
Chile	Copihue, lapageria rosea
Egypt	Lotus
England	Rose
France	Fleur de lis (Iris)
Germany	Cornflower
Greece	Violet
Holland	Tulip
India	Lotus
Ireland	Shamrock
Italy	Poppy or White Lily
Japan	Chrysanthemum
Malaysia	Hibiscus

Mexico	Vopal Cactus or Prickly Pear
Nepal	Rhododendron
New Zealand	Kowhai
Persia	Rose
Scotland	Thistle
Singapore	Orchid:
South Africa	Protea
Spain	Pomegranate Carnation
Switzerland	Edelweiss
United States	American Rose
Wales	Leek and Daffodil
Zimbabwe	Flame Lily

Here is a list of state flowers of USA
Alabama - Camellia
Alaska - Forget Me Not
Arizona - Saguaro Cactus
Arkansas - Apple Blossom
California - Golden Poppy
Colorado - Columbine
Connecticut - Mountain Laurel
Delaware - Peach Blossom
Florida - Orange Blossom
Georgia - Cherokee Rose
Hawaii - Yellow Hibiscus
Idaho - Syringa
Illinois - Native Violet
Indiana - Peony
Iowa - Wild Rose
Kansas - Sunflower
Kentucky - Goldenrod
Louisiana - Magnolia
Maine - White Pine Cone
Maryland - Black Eyed Susan
Massachusetts - May flower
Michigan - Apple Blossom
Minnesota - Lady Slipper
Mississippi - Magnolia
Missouri - Hawthorn
Montana - Bitterroot
Nebraska - Goldenrod
Nevada - Sagebrush
New Hampshire - Purple Lilac
New Jersey - Purple Violet
New Mexico - Yucca
New York - Rose

North Carolina - Dogwood
North Dakota - Wild Prairie Rose
Ohio - Scarlet Carnation
Oklahoma - Mistletoe
Oregon - Oregon Grape
Pennsylvania - Mountain Laurel
Rhode Island - Violet
South Carolina - Yellow Jessamine
South Dakota - Pasque Flower
Tennessee - Iris
Texas - Blue Bonnet
Utah - Sego Lily
Vermont - Red Clover
Virginia - Dogwood
Washington - Rhododendron
West Virginia - Big Rhododendron
Wisconsin - Wood Violet
Wyoming - Indian Paintbrush

Bouquet of Love©

Chapter 8

Do You Have a Witch Hazel Tree in Your Yard or Woods?

As I deal with the gardens in my old age, I still feel the need to have something different or better still, I feel it is important to plant something that will outlast me. I came across a picture of some Witch Hazel blossoms the other day and it started me thinking about it.

If you walk in the woods during the fall and winter, you may come across a small tree with fragrant yellow blossoms. Does this plant has its seasons mixed up and "thinks" its spring? Well, you have just come across a witch hazel, which is a small tree belonging to the plant family Hamamelidaceae and related to the sweet gum.

Further investigation taught me that witch hazels are not a large family, and perhaps this is one of the reasons for their remarkable under use in our landscapes.

Native to North America and parts of Asia, the first member to come to prominence in the garden was the American variety *Hamamelis virginiana*, discovered growing wild in Eastern woodlands early in the 1700s.

Brought to England in 1736, it was immediately prized, not for its flowers, which are rather small, but for its season of bloom -- it is the very last plant to flower in the garden, often opening into December -- hence its nickname "Epiphany Tree." Native Americans, on the other hand, had long valued the shrub for additional reasons: They were the first to understand that the inner bark had astringent qualities and used witch hazel as an effective cure for various inflammations of the skin and eyes. Witch hazel remains an ingredient in many commercial cosmetic preparations today.

Illinois has one native species of witch hazel, *Hamamelis virginiana*, which grows in colonies in the under story of dry or moist woods. The plant seldom reaches more then 10 feet tall and can be identified by its scallop-margined leaves that turn brilliant yellow in the fall and are arranged alternatively on zigzagging branches. This allows each leaf maximum exposure to the sun filtering through its shady domain. The plant's blossoms appear after the leaves have fallen, forming yellow clusters along the branches. The flowers have four long strap-like petals, each an inch to an inch and a half long. These petals have the unique ability to curl up in a bud when the temperatures drop and unfurl in the warming sun. This adaptation protects the nectar and pollen for warmer days when insects will venture out again. Witch hazel flowers are followed by a hard, two-chambered seed capsule that ripens a year later.

Witch hazel is a plant with many common names, each related to a unique aspect of the plant. The generic name, Hamamelis, means "together with fruit," and refers to the fact that witch hazel is the only tree in the North American woods to have ripe fruit, flowers, and next year's leaf buds all on the branch at the same time. The name "snapping hazel" comes from the seedpods. As they dry and shrink, they will explode with an audible pop to scatter the seeds up to 30 feet from the parent. This mechanism for seed dispersal helps to eliminate overcrowding and increases the likelihood that this year's crop will have room to grow. The name *Hamamelis* was adopted from a Greek word to indicate its resemblance to an apple-tree.

The tree has also been called water-witch. The word witch comes from an Anglo-Saxon word meaning "to bend." The forked springy branches of witch hazel were used by early settlers, and later dowsers, as divining rods to search and detect underground water and minerals.

Native Americans showed the pioneer how to make extracts for use as eye washes, liniment, and to stop bleeding. Modern uses include an astringent made from the tannin-rich bark, twigs, and leaves to be used on insect bites, stings, sunburn, and as a soothing after-shave lotion. In the past, even the army has used branches of witch hazel for camouflage purposes.

The next time you take a walk in the woods watch out the witch hazel's yellow blossoms and popping seedpods as they bring a bit of a reprieve during those gray days of fall and winter.

It is synonymous with the Spotted Alder, Winterbloom, and Snapping Hazelnut. The bark, dried; leaves, fresh and dried are used and the Eastern United States and Canada is where it can be found. They also grow in Britain.

This shrub, long known in cultivation, consists of several crooked branching trunks from one root, 4 to 6 inches in diameter, 10 to 12 feet in height, with a smooth grey bark,  leaves 3 to 5 inches long and about 3 inches wide, on short petioles, alternate, oval shaped. The leaves drop off in autumn, and then the yellow flowers appear, very late in September and in October, in clusters from the joints, followed by black nuts, containing white seeds which are oily and edible. In Britain, the nut does not bear seeds, but in America, they are produced abundantly, but often do not ripen till the following summer. The seeds are ejected violently when ripe, hence the name Snapping Hazelnut. The alternative name "Snapping Hazel" hints at another: the tree ejects its seeds explosively into the air, insuring widespread propagation without overcrowding. And because it blossoms bright yellow in the darkening days of fall and winter, witch hazel is also called "Winterbloom."

The leaves are inodorous, with an astringent and bitter aromatic taste. Leaves are simple, alternate, deciduous, and asymmetrical with an unequal base, wavy margin and hair on the underside. Of the *leaves* (official in the United States Pharmacopoeia), tannic and Gallic acids, an unknown bitter principle and some volatile oil.

The twigs are flexible and rough, color externally, yellowish-brown to purple, wood greenly white, pith small. The bark as found in commerce is usually in quilted pieces 1/16 inch thick, 2 to 8 inches long, with silvery grey, scaly cork; longitudinally striated; fracture fibrous and laminated; taste and odor slight. Young twigs are hairy and buds are hairy and naked (without visible scales). Bark is light brown-gray and fairly smooth with lenticels. The flowers are yellow or reddish, thread-like, and bloom in autumn. The fruit is a woody capsule that ejects seeds in the winter. Witch-hazel is found in the under story of moist upland sites in the eastern U.S. and is tolerant of shade. Witch-hazel astringent is made from the inner bark. The fruit is eaten by birds and squirrels. So here is another fine reason for planting one or two on your property.

The *bark* contains tannin, partly amorphous and partly crystal, Gallic acid, a physterol, resin, fat and other bitter and odorous bodies. There are many medicinal uses for this plant. The properties of the leaves and bark are similar, astringent, tonic, sedative, and valuable in checking internal and external hemorrhage, most efficacious in the treatment of piles, a good pain-killer for the same, useful for bruises and inflammatory swellings, also for diarrhea, dysentery and mucous discharges.
It has long been used by the North American Indians as poultices for painful swellings and tumors.

A tea made of the leaves or bark may be taken freely with advantage, being good for bleeding of the stomach and in complaints of the bowels, and an injection of this tea is excellent for inwardly bleeding piles, the relief being marvelous and the cure speedy. An ointment made of 1 part fluid extract of bark to 9 parts simple ointment is also used as a local application, the concentration Hamamelin being also employed, mainly in the form of suppositories.

Witch Hazel has been supposed to owe its utility to an action on the muscular fiber of veins. The distilled extract from the fresh leaves and young twigs forms an excellent remedy for internal or external uses, being beneficial for bleeding from the lungs and nose, as well as from other internal organs. In the treatment of varicose veins, it should be applied on a lint bandage, which must be constantly kept moist: a pad of Witch Hazel applied to a burst varicose vein will stop the bleeding and often save life by its instant application.

Witch Hazel was much used in our grandmother's days as a general household remedy for burns, scalds, and inflammatory conditions of the skin generally and it is still in general use. I find it has an immediate affect on piles. Here is some other information I discovered for its uses. Remember to check with your doctor first.

In cases of bites of insects and mosquitoes a pad of cotton-wool, moistened with the extract and applied to the spot will soon cause the pain and swelling to subside.
Diluted with warm water, the extract is used for inflammation of the eyelids.

Liquor Hamamelidis, 1/2 to 3 drachms (a distillate of the fresh leaves). Used also with equal parts of glycerin as injection for piles.
Liquid extract, 5 to 15 minims (preparation of the dried leaves made with alcohol) externally for varicose veins. Injection for piles, 2 to 5 minims.
Hamamelin, 1/2 to 2 grains, in pill (powdered extractive from the bark). 1 to 3 grains with cacao butter is useful for piles.
Tincture (from the bark), 30 to 60 minims. 1 drachma in 3 OZ. cold water given as enema for piles. Lotion of 1 or 2 drachms with water to an ounce useful for bruises.
Ointment: employed externally for piles.

Witch Hazel trees will easily grow in zones 4 to 8 in any kind of widely adaptable soil. They can be bought from most local and on line nurseries. Their prices usually start around $16.00 for small trees or plants. Their growth is slow, so should you get a small plant, you may have to nurture it though a bigger potting session before you put it where you finally want it. It grows in both full sun and full shade and it deals with widely adaptable moisture. As I said their growth is slow, and in fact remains slow throughout the life of the tree in its typical shady habitat. As individuals, witch-hazel probably does not live more than 100 years, but they reproduce from root sprouts, and clones may live for a very long time.

Maybe I'll order a couple for posterity!

Buddha's Umbrella©

Chapter 9

How to Divide Cannas

Three or four years ago I planted 3 Cannas Rhizomes in one part of my garden and 3 in another part.

On July 25, 2005, I was sitting on my patio having breakfast and looked out over the cottage garden to see masses of Cannas. I thought, "What a fantastic plant for hiding just about anything. Tall dense clumps of large heavy foliage make perfect screens or wonderful backdrops and grows practically anywhere."

However, they were now where I really did not want them. They were blocking lots of vision. I will have to live with them until next spring since that is the time to deal with them.

We are in zone 6 and they just come back every year. In cooler areas plants die back in winter but readily re-grow once warm weather returns. They are a clump forming bush that are excellent used mass planted for a showy flower display or used as individual specimens interplanted with other trees and shrubs in your garden.

Cannas, or cannas lilies, look like banana trees without the trunk! That's no accident - they're kin to bananas and gingers, and their wide, furled leaves come out of thick, multiple-eyed rhizomes, just like their larger, edible cousins. Flowers are the main reason cannas are so highly prized, though.

The tropical Indian shot (*Canna indica*) was hybridized and backcrossed with other *Canna* species, including the North American native, golden Canna. These hybrids have been known as *Canna* X *generalis*, or *Canna* X *orchiodes*, depending on flower characteristics, but they've been crossed too, and the distinctions are now largely lost or forgotten.

Nowadays most experts include all the cannas hybrids under *Canna* X *generalis*. And indeed there are hundreds of named cultivars, ranging from less than 30 in (76.2 cm) to more than 8 ft (2.4 m) in height, in colors from creams to yellows, to oranges and reds, and with a colorful diversity of leaf patterns as well. Some of the most striking cultivars have red or variegated foliage. Cannas flowers are asymmetrical, with three petals, three sepals and three highly modified showy petal-like stamens. They come in a rainbow of shades from yellows, oranges, reds and pinks. The flowers are followed by a capsule with round, shot like seeds.

Canna flaccida is native to the southeastern U.S. and Central America and the Antilles. *Canna indica* is native to tropical Central and South America. The many hybrid selections are of garden origin, some dating back to the 18th century. Cannas species and various hybrids have naturalized in wetlands throughout the subtropical and tropical world.

Cannas are an upright clump forming plant that will add spectacular color to your garden. They are ideal used in tropical style gardens, mass planted for dramatic flower color and are great used interplanted with other trees and shrubs. Cannas are a very hardy plant and can withstand wetter areas and periods of dryness. Cannas prefer sun, but will grow in partial shade.

Cannas like moist soil and will thrive even in boggy conditions. They can be grown in ordinary garden soils, but will need regular watering.

USDA Zones 8-12. Cannas can be grown in colder regions, but where the ground freezes, either lift the rhizomes during winter, or protect them with a thick layer of mulch. In cold climates, the rhizomes may be susceptible to rot.

Cannas are easy to propagate by dividing off pieces of the rhizomes.

There are just 9 species of *Cannas*, all native to the New World tropics and subtropics. *Canna indica*, also known as *Canna edulis*, makes an edible root and is the source of arrowroot starch. Its seeds have been used as shot (thus the common name, "Indian shot"). *A canna is* from the Greek for a type of reed.

Cannas are beautiful tropical plants that are hardy to Zone 9. In colder parts of the country, they need to be dug up just after the first frost in the fall and stored indoors in a cool, dark location. Leaving soil on the rhizomes helps keep them from shriveling up. Also, cutting the rhizome before storage could let organisms in that cause rot, so it's better left whole. In the spring, though, you may want to divide them.

I never realized that Cannas lilies are remarkably easy to grow. These are great flowers for a wet area. They will even grow in moderately polluted wetlands. Cannas look best in masses. Leaf rolling caterpillars can be devastating to the foliage, but are easily controlled. Plant cannas with bananas, gingers and palms for an enormous tropical foliage statement!

To divide a cannas rhizome, brush off the dried soil so that you can see eyes, or buds. Cut off any old foliage. Use a sharp knife, cut the rhizome so that there are two to three healthy eyes on each division.

Plant the cannas in a sunny spot after the danger of frost has passed in the spring. Bury the rhizomes, eyes up, about six inches deep, spaced 12 inches apart. Plant them where they have room to spread because they do. They will come up between cracks in walkways. I know, I have them in our walkways.

You can plant cannas in the back of your garden for a tall border. They also do well in pots in sunny locations if you take care to water them well.

Plant just below soil surface. This plant is very effective and showy in groups. Canna foliage acts as a great cover along fence lines and walls. In cooler climates cut all growth back to 10-12 inches above ground level in early winter. In very cold areas protect rhizomes against frost with a layer of mulch. Cannas can be left undisturbed for many years given they are fertilized sufficiently as they become crowded.

Family: Cannaceae (kan-AY-see-ay)
Genus: Canna (KAN-uh)
Species: *x generalis* (jen-er-RAY-liss)

Category:
Perennials

Height:
4-6 ft. (1.2-1.8 m)

Spacing:
9-12 in. (22-30 cm)

Hardiness:
USDA Zone 7b: to -14.9° C (5° F)
USDA Zone 8a: to -12.2° C (10° F)
USDA Zone 8b: to -9.4° C (15° F)
USDA Zone 9a: to -6.6° C (20° F)
USDA Zone 9b: to -3.8° C (25° F)
USDA Zone 10a: to -1.1°C (30° F)
USDA Zone 10b: to 1.7° C (35° F)
USDA Zone 11: above 4.5° C (40° F)

Sun Exposure:
Full Sun

Chapter 10

How to Care for Crape Myrtle

When your crape myrtle starts to flower, the hot weather is setting in.

I do not know a lot about crape myrtle and I have two large bushes that I keep doing things to that probably defies all the laws of gardening, but they keep coming back.

I live in zone 6. Our daughter, Glynis, has just moved here from zone 7 and the street she lived on was loaded with crape myrtle in the form of sidewalk trees of all colors. It is a lovely street. So the note below about zone 7 may or may not be correct. Perhaps all those houses on that city street keep the air warm in the winter time for the crape myrtles.

Here is the research I have done on crape myrtles.

After the first flush of blooms fade, cut off the flowers and apply a light fertilizer for a repeat (but smaller) bloom. If crape myrtles fail to bloom for you, it could be due to too much shade, hard winter-type pruning performed too late in the season, or having too short of a growing season.

Depending on your personal tastes, consider these options:
- They are normally multi-trunked and respond well to pollarding, an old European way of hard pruning that produces a beautiful umbrella-like effect. However, once started, you must continue this method for the remainder of the life of the tree.

- They can be grown as standards with a rounded top, and will reach from 10 to 20 feet high. They are effective in groups, or as specimens.

- Mildew resistant varieties usually bear Indian names, such as 'Catawba' (purple), 'Cherokee' (bright red), 'Muskogee (light lavender), 'Potomac' (pink) , 'Powhatan', 'Seminole', 'Tuscadora', my favorite, (coral pink), and 'Natchez', (white, 25 ft).

- Semi-dwarf varieties (6 to 10 feet) are 'Acoma' (white), 'Hopi' (pink), 'Pecos' (pink), and 'Zuni' (lavender). And dwarf varieties are also available to 4 feet. Vibrant fall color and lovely winter bark are a bonus.

If you're at the northern end of zone 7, your crape myrtles could die to the ground. Most crape myrtles are root-hardy as far north as Massachusetts if well mulched in winter, however, expect vigorous growth and blossoming by late spring to early summer. Select a planting site with a southern exposure, and/or a protected area such as a wall or steep embankment. *Lagerstroemia* 'fauriei' is a newly developed hybrid that performs much better in colder climes, and blooms earlier in the season.

Propagation via seed is easy, and seedlings often bloom the first year. You'll need a month of cold stratification (a Ziploc baggy kept in the fridge will do it) for easy success.

Cuttings are easily rooted, and will be true to parent varieties; but may not bloom until their second year.

Crape myrtles are being planted in pecan orchards for their properties of attracting and sustaining beneficial insects, and can serve the same purpose in the home landscape.

Contrary to many resources that claim these plants to be disease and pest-free, if you're in a humid climate expect powdery mildew and aphids. However, don't jump the gun on insecticides; the crape myrtle aphid is host-specific to only crape myrtles, but is the preferred diet of 30 or so of our best beneficial insect predators. To destroy the crape myrtle aphid is to deprive your garden of a host of natural predators.

Touted by entomologists as probably the most important landscape plant in the southeastern U.S., crape myrtles are being planted in pecan orchards for their properties of attracting and sustaining beneficial insects, and can serve the same purpose in the home landscape.

Flowering occurs on new growth, so winter pruning is necessary for best results. Vigorous root systems wreak havoc on anything but the most persistent perennial underplantings and groundcovers. *Liriope* 'Big Blue' makes a lovely ground cover underneath, blossoming simultaneously.

If you're lucky enough to grow crape myrtle, look forward not only to weeks of hot weather and colorful bloom, but a safety net of predator insects.

Chapter 11

How to Prune Flowering Shrubs

1. Removing spent flowers also removes berries that might form for birds later in the season. Determine the best time for pruning (and if they even need it) so the birds aren't denied the berries.
2. Make sure that it is the correct time of the season to prune (see Related Features below).
3. Use sharpened tools that are large enough to do the job.
4. Use shears only for formal hedges; most flowering shrubs look best when left in a natural shape.
5. Use loppers and/or pruners for a natural look.
6. Remove dead and diseased branches at the place of their origination. Do not leave a stub.
7. Cut crossing branches that rub against each other.
8. Cut branches growing toward the center of the plant.

First remove dead and diseased branches.

Cut crossing branches that rub against each other.

Make the final pruning cut into healthy wood.

Make cuts at an angle so that water runs off of them.

Refrain from shearing a plant into a box shape; over time, the top will dominate with few lower branches and foliage due to the difference in light.

Never remove more than one third of the total plant; if something is overgrown, prune it over time for best results.

Abelia - selective thinning of damaged and crowded stems in spring. In severe winter areas, may be cut back severely and mulched in early winter.

Althaea (Rose of Sharon), Shrub Althaea- where winters are warm, prune in winter. Otherwise, wait until early spring. Selective pruning during the first two years; thereafter cut 3 year old wood back to the ground.

Azalea - prune after flowering. Remove faded blossoms before they seed for a better flower display the following year.

Barberry - late spring, thin and shape for hedge or topiary.

Beautyberry - prune before spring growth begins.

Bridal-wreath spirea *(Spiraea prunifolia)* - blooms on previous years growth; prune in spring after flowers fade. When overgrown, remove oldest stems at the base.

Buddleia - if it didn't get killed to the ground, leave only 4-5 inch stems with 2 or more buds on *Buddleia alternifolia*, which blooms on previous year's growth. *Buddleia davidii* (summer lilac, butterfly bush) can be cut back to the ground. Pinch tips of new growth for more vigorous plants. In temperate areas, cut back to 3 feet in late fall.

Camellia - prune before spring growth begins.

Chinese Hibiscus *(Hibiscus rosa-sinensis)* - remove one third of old wood in early spring if not killed to the ground.

Cotoneaster - prune in early spring; thin out by removing older stems if needed. Prune tips to control growth.

Deutzia - prune after flowering; cut 3 year old wood to the ground and remove weak, spindly growth.

Firethorn *(Pyracantha)* - remove fruited branches in early spring; prune to control shape and size.

Flowering Quince - prune after flowering.

Forsythia - after blooming in spring, remove 4 year old wood (older branches) at the base of the plant. Leave the younger arching branches.

French Hydrangea *(Hydrangea macrophylla)* - blooms on old wood; prune after flowering by removing old canes. Cut stems that flowered back to next laterals.

Honeysuckle, woodbine *(Lonicera)* - prune after spring flowering. Remove 2 year old stems at ground level.

Lilac *(Syringa)* - blooms on previous year's growth; prune oldest branches at ground level after flowers fade. Remove seed pods, dead & diseased wood, and suckers growing from grafts at the base.

Mock Orange *(Philadelphus)* - prune after bloom in spring by removing 3 year old wood to the ground. Cut back flowering branches to a lateral.

Modern Roses - prune before spring growth begins.

Mountain Laurel *(Kalmia)* - prune after bloom in spring

Nandina - prune before spring growth begins

Old Garden Roses - prune after flowering

Rhododendrons - prune immediately after bloom

Sweetshrub, strawberry bush *(Calycanthus floridus)* - prune before spring growth begins

Tamarisk *(Tamarisk ramosissima)* - prune severely in spring; also clip flowers after they fade

Tea Olive *(Osmanthus fragrans)* - prune before spring growth begins

Weigela- After flowers fade; prune flowering branches to the next lateral. Remove dead wood to the ground.

Winter Daphne - prune after flowering

Wisteria - prune after flowering, by pinching; many prune in winter for more foliage. Root pruning is also an effective means of control.

1. Make final cuts into healthy wood.
2. Make cuts at an angle so water runs off of them.
3. If shearing a formal hedge into a box or ball shape, leave the plant slightly wider at the bottom, or the bottom growth will die back from lack of light.

Simply put, prune the following after flowering:

Azalea
Beautybush Bigleaf Hydrangea
Bradford Pear
Bridalwreath Spirea
Clematis
Climbing Roses
Crabapple
Deutzia
Dogwood
Doublefile Vibernum
Flowering Almond
Flowering Cherry
Flowering Quince
Forsythia
Japanese Kerria
Japanese Pieris
Lilac
Mockorange
Oakleaf Hydrangea
Pearlbush

Pyracantha
Redbud
Saucer Magnolia
Star Magnolia
Shrub Honeysuckle
Thunberg Spirea
Vanhoutte Spirea
Weigelia
Winter Daphne
Wisteria
Witchhazel

Prune the following before Spring growth begins: Beautyberry
Camellia
Goldenrain Tree
Chaste Tree (Vitex)
Cranberrybush Viburnum
Crape myrtle
Floribunda Roses
Fragrant Tea Olive
Gloss Abelia
Grandiflora Roses
Japanese Barberry
Japanese Spirea
Mimosa
Nandina
Rose-of-Sharon (Althea)
Sourwood
Anthony Waterer Spirea
Sweetshrub

Birdwing Butterfly©

Chapter 12

Every Garden Needs Deer Resistant Plants

Sure it looks nice to see those deer out in your garden eating up your money. Eating your money? That's exactly what they do when you allow them to eat your plants!

When you first start your flower garden make sure you buy perennials that are deer resistant, drought resistant and care free.

When you first start your vegetable garden, make sure you put a very high fence around it or put some deer resistant perennials around it because those pesky critters will be up bright and early before you are having their breakfast at your expense!

So I am providing the following for your guidelines:

A Partial List of Deer-resistant Garden Plants
Botanical Name and Common Name of Ground Covers
Ajuga reptans Carpet Bugle
Convallaria majalis Lily-of-the-Valley
Lamium spp. Dead Nettle
Pachysandra terminalis Pachysandra
Vinca major Large Periwinkle
Vinca minor Periwinkle

Botanical Name and Common Name of Flowers
Achillea spp. Yarrow
Aquilegia spp. Columbine
Astilbe spp. Astilbe
Coreopsis spp. Tickseed
Dianthus spp. Pinks
Dicentra spp. Bleeding Heart
Digitalis spp. Foxglove
Echinacea spp. Purple Coneflower
Epimedium spp. Epimedium
Eupatorium purpureum Bluestem Joe-Pye-Weed
Geranium spp. Cranesbill, Geranium
Helleborus spp. Hellebore
Helianthus spp. Sunflower
Iberis spp. Candytuft
Iris spp. Iris
Lavendula spp. Lavender
Liatris spicata Spike Gay-Feather

Lychnis coronaria Rose Campion
Narcissus spp. Daffodil
Pulmonaria spp. Lungwort
Rudbechia spp. Coneflower
Solidago spp. Goldenrod
Veronica officinalis Speedwell
Yucca filimentosa Yucca

Botanical Name and Common Name of Vines
Celastrus spp. Bittersweet
Clematis spp. Clematis
Hedera helix baltica Baltic Ivy
Lonicera spp. Honeysuckle

Botanical Name and Common Name of Shrubs
Amorpha canescens Lead Plant
Berberis Koreana Korean Barberry
Berberis thunbergii Japanese Barberry
Caragana arborescens
'Sutherland' Sutherland Caragana
Caragana arborescens
'Lorbergi' Fernleaf Caragana
Caragana aurantiaca Pygmy Caragana
Caragana frutex Russian Caragana
Caragana frutex Dwarf Russian
Globosa Caragana

A Partial List of Deer-resistant Garden Plants

Botanical Name Common Name
Caragana Maximowicz
Maximowicziana Caragana
Caragana pekinensis Pekinese Caragana
Ceanothus velutinus Snowbush Ceanothus
Cornus sericea Red Osier Dogwood
Cornus stolonifera Osier Dogwood
Eleagnus angustifolia Russian Olive
Eleagnus commutata Silverberry
Halimodendron halodendron Siberian Salt Tree
Juniperus chinensis Chinese Juniper
Juniperus chinensis 'Hetzii' Hetz Juniper
Juniperus communis
'Vase Shape' Vase common Juniper
Juniperus horizontalis
Plumosa Compact Andorra Juniper
Juniperus horizontalis

'Lividus' Lividus Creeping Juniper
Juniperus sabina
'Von Ehron' Von Ehron Savin Juniper
Kolkwitzia amabilis Beautybush
Lonicera spp. Honeysuckle
Philadelphus spp. Mockorange
Prunus Americana American plum
Prunus fruticosa Groundcherry
Prunus tenella Dwarf Russian Almond
Rosa rugosa Rugose rose
Rosa virginiana Virginia Rose
Rosa wichuraiana Memorial Rose
Rosa 'Betty Bland' Betty Bland Rose
Rosa 'Haidee' Haidee Rose
Rhus trilobata Fragrant Sumac
Rhamnus cathartica Common Buckthorn
Sheperdia argentea Buffaloberry
Spiraea spp. Bridalwreath
Syringa villosa Late Lilac
Syringa vulgaris Common Lilac
Viburnum opulus Highbush Cranberry
Yucca filamentosa Adam's Needle

Botanical Name and Common Name of Trees
Acer platanoides Norway maple
Acer saccharinum Silver Maple
Betula papyrifera Paper Birch
Betula pendula European White Birch
Crataegus spp. Hawthorn
Galitsis triathlons Honey Locust
Picea abies Norway spruce
Picea glauca White Spruce
Picea pungens Colorado Blue Spruce
Pinus nigra Austrian Pine
Pinus mugho Mugo Pine
Pinus sylvestris Scotch Pine
Tsuga canadensis Canada Hemlock

Chapter 13

So You're Thinking of Planting an Apple Orchard

(Apple paintings by Arlene Wright-Correll)

Fall is upon us and so is the wonderful season of fresh apples

Planting an apple orchard or any kind of orchard is a wonderful idea whether it is a large orchard or a small one. Regardless, have a plan. Stake out your area. Plant in the fall and dig your holes twice the size of the root ball. Make sure you buy for your area and from a reputable fruit tree nursery which will give you a good guarantee on your trees. Seriously consider dwarf fruit trees since they will produce quicker, be easier to maintain. Make sure you have cross pollinators if you need them. Consider putting in some bee hives. If you live in a windy area like we do you will have to stake them down for about 4 years or they will all be listing to one side.

This chapter will ramble on about apples because I love them. There are all kinds of apples and all kinds of information about apples and last but not least what to do with your apple crop so I am including some of my favorite recipes.

Apples are the 2nd largest crop production in the United States with oranges being the first. Wherever apples grow you can be sure some critter will be enjoying their goodness and flavor. From raccoons and bears, to horses and insects, as they love apples as much as humans do and we do love apples since the apple tree is the most widely cultivated of all the fruit trees

This is proved by the world apple production statistics. In 1997, an amazing 44.7 million metric tons of apples were produced for human consumption. Of those, more than 84% were bought and used commercially (by a company).

In the United States, 4.6 million metric tons of apples were produced in 1997, with a wholesale value of more than $1 billion (U.S.). Of those apples, roughly:

- 50% were enjoyed as fresh fruit.
- 20% were used to make vinegar, cider, wine, juice, jelly, and apple butter.
- 17% were canned as applesauce and pie filling.
- 13% were exported (sold to other countries).

Although people across the United States love apples, apples grow particularly well in the cooler northern states. Washington State is the leading apple-producing state, followed by Michigan, and New York. A trip to Yakama Valley is worth it, even upstate New York.

The leading apple growing country is China, producing about 41% of the world's apples, followed by the United States, Turkey, France, Poland, Italy, the Russian Federation, Germany, Argentina, Japan, and Chile. Even warmer countries like Iraq and Mexico are able to grow apples in their cooler upland regions.

We Americans have a favorite story about a pioneer apple farmer named John Chapman, from Leominster, Massachusetts. Chapman, now known to many as "Johnny Appleseed", became famous in the 1800's when he distributed apple seeds and trees to settlers in the American states of Ohio, Indiana, and Illinois. Legend claims that Appleseed traveled barefoot wearing old torn clothes and a tin pot for a hat! Johnny Appleseed is celebrated in American folklore as a symbol of the westward-moving expansion of the European settlers.

The apple is our Canadian neighbor's most important fruit crop. Canadian growers produced about 506,000 metric tons of apples in 1997, worth about $182 million (Canadian). Our leading apple producing province is Ontario, followed by British Columbia, Quebec, Nova Scotia, and New Brunswick. More than 7,000 Canadian farms grow apples on over 30,000 hectares of farmland.

The first trees to produce sweet, flavorful apples similar to those we enjoy today, were located many thousands of years ago near the modern city of Alma-Ata, Kazakhstan.

The Greeks were growing several varieties of apples by the late 300's BC, and the ancient Romans also grew and loved the fruit. Researchers have even found the charred remains of apples at a Stone Age village in Switzerland.

European settlers brought apple seeds and trees with them to the New World. Records from the Massachusetts Bay Company indicate that apples were being grown in New England as early as 1630. In 1796, in Ontario, Canada, John McIntosh discovered a variety of apple which is today enjoyed by people around the world

John McIntosh came to Canada with the United Empire Loyalists, a group of people forced to flee the United States during the 1770's because they remained loyal to Britain during the American Revolution.

McIntosh spent time on the frontier before settling in Dundas County, Ontario, Canada, in 1790. The town where he settled was later called McIntosh's Corners, and is now called Dundela.

While clearing some land in 1796, McIntosh discovered about 20 young apple trees. He transplanted the trees to a place near his home, but by 1830, only one tree was still alive. McIntosh combined his own name with the color of the fruit, and called the tree the "McIntosh Red".

From the time the tree was first transplanted it produced an abundance of tasty apples. In 1893, the McIntosh house caught fire and the tree, located just 15 feet from the house, was badly burned along one side. However, the healthy side continued to produce apples until 1908.

Fortunately, as early as 1836, McIntosh's son Allan began grafting parts of the tree so that it could be grown in other places by other farmers.

Two monuments stand at Dundela commemorating McIntosh and his wonderful apple.

Apples have also appeared in legends in our past. In the Bible, Adam and Eve are tempted by apples in the Garden of Eden, and in the Swiss story of William Tell, an archer is arrested and then promised his freedom if he can shoot an apple off his son's head with an arrow.

Apple trees grow in the temperate regions of the world (areas that don't get too hot or too cold), generally in the latitudes between 30° to 60° north and south. Apple trees are best adapted to places where the average winter temperature is near freezing for at least two months, though many varieties can withstand winter temperatures as low as -40°C (-40°F).

Apple trees are deciduous, which means their leaves fall off at the end of the growing season.

Apple trees belong to the Rosaceae (rose) family, and in the spring you can see the beautiful white flowers on an apple tree looking like tiny roses. Taxonomists (scientists that name and classify living things) have called the cultivated species of apple tree *Malus domestica*, and the wild species *Malus pumila*.

Apples come in thousands of varieties, sizes, textures, and tastes.

The color of the outside of an apple may be green, yellow, or various shades of red. Some yellow apples have weird brown spots all over them, while some red apples, like the Jonathan, have even weirder white spots! Apple colors also differ on the inside, where the flesh may be yellow, white, or cream-colored. It's also interesting that apples will turn brown if you cut them open and leave them out for a couple of hours.

Each variety of apple has a slightly different flavor, from sweet, to tart, to bitter, to—what each of us consider is just right!

Textures also vary amongst apple varieties, from soft and mushy, to firm and crunchy.

Because there are so many different varieties of apple, each with slightly different qualities than the next, producers grow different types of apples for different purposes. Some apples, like the Empire, are sweet and wonderful when eaten fresh (in fact, of all the cultivated apples grown, over half are eaten fresh). Other apple varieties are better suited for cooking or further processing. The Rome Beauty, for example, is often used for baking and not eaten fresh because it has a firm, acidic flesh, and tough, smooth skin.

In 1999, our late son, Fred and I planted a small apple orchard here at Home Farm. They are different varieties and are all dwarf apple trees. These trees are just starting to bear some fruit now. Most of the dwarf apple trees get truly abundant produce about 10 to 16 years of age. Apple trees grow in the temperate regions of the world (areas that don't get too hot or too cold), generally in the latitudes between 30° to 60° north and south. Apple trees are best adapted to places where the average winter temperature is near freezing for at least two months, though many varieties can withstand winter temperatures as low as -40°C (-40°F).

Apple trees are deciduous, which means their leaves fall off at the end of the growing season and what looks lovelier than seeing the apple blossoms in the spring.

Apple trees belong to the Rosaceae (rose) family, and in the spring you can see the beautiful white flowers on an apple tree looking like tiny roses. Taxonomists (scientists that name and classify living things) have called the cultivated species of apple tree *Malus domestica*, and the wild species *Malus pumila*.

Apples are healthy for you. I can remember as a child, my grandmother always telling me, "An apple a day, keeps the doctor away!" Both the American Produce for Better Health Foundation and the National Cancer Institute of America recommend a minimum of 5 servings of fruit per day to maintain a healthy diet. Part of this should definitely be composed of yummy apples! Believe it or not, 1 medium-sized apple contains no fat, cholesterol, or sodium (salt). It also gives you more fiber than a serving of oatmeal. The seeds have a bit of deadly hydrogen cyanide in them.

I remember when we lived in Northern N.Y., we used to go to old farms that had abandoned orchards and pick bushels of apples. Then we would take them to an old fellow who had a gasoline driven apple crusher. He would crush and press our apples on 50/50 shares. It was a great family fun weekend. Picking apples one day and crushing the next. What wonderful cider and we had plenty. We were able to make wonderful sparkling apple wine.

Surveys have shown that **survey also found** that 100 percent apple juice is the fruit juice most often recommended as the first juice for infants. Parents are good about this with babies, but somewhere along the way the researchers found the following: "Research from the University of Florida's Institute of Food and Agricultural Sciences adds strong evidence to an ongoing debate about consumption of 100% fruit juice and finds that fruit juice consumption is *not* linked with problems related to overweight and growth problems in children.

After analyzing beverage consumption of more than 10,000 children from various age groups, the researchers found that while most children are within guidelines established by the American Academy of Pediatrics for juice intake, children's consumption of less nutritious beverages surpasses their intake of 100 percent juice as early as age 5.

"Consuming 100 percent fruit juice has been positively associated with children achieving recommended nutrient intakes," said Miami-based registered dietitian and ADA spokesperson Sheah Rarback. The research also identifies that at around age 7, children's consumption of 100 percent real juice flat-lines and is replaced with beverages that have significantly less or no nutritional value."

Apple products have a nutrient/calorie ratio superior to many of the alternative snacks being consumed by children. One serving of apple juice (4-6 ounces) or unsweetened applesauce (1/2 cup) serves as a fruit exchange, according to the meal planning guidelines published jointly by the American Dietetic Association and American Diabetes Association. Similarly, the U.S. Department of Agriculture's (USDA) Food Guide Pyramid states that 100% juice can be substituted for other fruits.

Well, parents, apples and 100% apple juice will keep your children well from cradle to grave, so why not put apples and 100% apple juice back into their children's diets? It's cheaper than soda and healthier for them. In the fall, we can usually find fresh apple cider most anywhere. A fun day is to take the whole family out to a "U pick" apple orchard and most times you will find each place has a cooler that looks like this. Sliced apples and peanut butter are a great kid's snack and we continue to eat that to this day at the ripe old age of 70.

As a child, I can remember parties where a large galvanized iron tub was filled with water and apples, which had a dime, penny, or quarter stuck into them, would bob around this big tub of water. We children would get down on our hands and knees and "bob for apples" trying to catch one with our teeth. No stems were allowed on the apples. Most times one had to put one's head into the water and push the apple clear to the bottom to gain purchase with one's teeth. I can remember even doing this game at my 16 year old surprise birthday party given for me by my school chums.

Due to the diverse variety of apples, harvesting occurs at different times throughout the year. Most apples in the U.S., however, are harvested in the fall (between August and October).

Before harvesting occurs, apples must be tested for "maturity" to determine if they're ready to be picked. This process allows consumers to receive fresh apples of the highest quality and for processors to select only the ripest apples for apple juice and applesauce. Apples that are harvested too early may taste sour or starchy, and apples harvested too late may be soft.

To determine maturity, many characteristics of the apples are checked prior to picking. The amount of sugar, the apple's firmness, seed, and skin color

Once the apples are confirmed to be "mature," they are picked (mostly by hand, although some mechanical methods have been developed). The apples are then placed in canvas bags or lined buckets inside of large bins. These apple-filled bins are picked up by a forklift, loaded onto a truck and transported to a central loading area - where apples that are bruised, cut or have insect or disease problems are immediately removed. The remaining apples are stored immediately to ensure maximum storage life.

The apples are now ready for the trip to your local grocery store or to be used in everyone's favorites: APPLE JUICE and APPLESAUCE.

Just like apples that are delivered fresh to your local grocery store, apples that are processed to make apple juice, applesauce and other apple products are picked at their optimum maturity. Only high quality, ripe apples will do! Apples that are an "off" shape or appear to have "skin blemishes" may not be ideal for the produce department - but they are perfectly suitable for processing.

Before raw apples are processed into apple juice, cider or sauce, they undergo extensive washing procedures designed to remove external surface dirt and topical agrichemical residues. Once the apples are cleaned and processed into apple juice or applesauce, they then are subject to analysis using sophisticated, government-approved testing methods that can monitor for even trace amounts of pesticide residues (or other agrichemicals). Apple processors always employ strict testing procedures, both in-house and through independent testing laboratories, to ensure the highest quality, purity and safety of their products. Even though apples undergo vigorous cleaning processes, it is possible that some residues may remain after processing. However, the amounts are so small as to be considered insignificant by strict government standards.

Every time I see apples in the store or at a fruit stand, I make it an issue to try a variety that I have never had before. I love crisp, juicy, apples, especially ones that are tart, while Carl's favorites a golden delicious, Rome apples or any others that are less juicy and sweeter.

There are some many varieties of apples in the world today and coming from so many places that it is often possible to have them fresh all year long. One just has to read the label on the apple to tell what country it is from. Other countries do not have the strict pesticide rules that we have here in the United States. With that in mind, I peel every apple I eat. I do not know whether or not that helps, but it makes me feel better.

One of my favorites is the Gala apple. Gala is a strikingly attractive apple. The bright yellow skin is finely stippled with red, as if airbrushed, and the result is near-neon intensity. From across a room you'd think you were looking at a peach. Gala was developed in New Zealand by J. H. Kidd, crossing Golden Delicious and his own Kidd's Orange Red. The work was done in the 1920s, but the apple wasn't named and introduced until the 1960s.

The pale, creamy yellow flesh is crisp and dense, with a mild, sweet flavor and good aroma. The fruit is not large, and especially small Galas are cleverly marketed here as lunchbox size. In taste tests Gala easily outscores McIntosh and is considered sprightlier than Golden Delicious. Tom Vorbeck of Applesource says that a typical first comment of people biting into one is "Best apple I ever had in my life." When cooked, Gala strikes some people as bland, but it can be dried with good results. Gala is also used in cider blends.

Fruits imported from New Zealand first appear in stores from August and on into October; your refrigerator will stretch the life of the apples another three or four months.

Only recently I discovered the Jonagold over at Jackson's Orchard in Bowling Green, KY. The fortunes of Jonagold reveal much about national differences in apple appreciation. Although released in 1968 by New York State's Geneva Station, this cross of Jonathan and Golden Delicious has succeeded far better in Europe than at home. Large plantings have been made in Britain, France, Italy, Switzerland, and Belgium - Jonagold may become Europe's number one apple - as well as in Japan. But the home crowd resists it, preferring the familiar red, sweet, tame Red Delicious. It has been said that Americans eat apples with their eyes, and Jonagold is a case in point.

Nevertheless, this variety is the leading apple west of the Cascades in Washington State, and in British Columbia Jonagold challenges McIntosh as the number one variety.

With its aroma of Golden Delicious and the sprightliness of Jonathan, Jonagold is an excellent sweet-tart dessert apple. The texture of the creamy yellow flesh is noticeably crisp and juicy. In a poll of nineteen apple experts in nine countries, Jonagold scored as the overall favorite. The fruit makes fair sauce and a good pie.

Harvest varies from mid-September to late October. The apples keep well unless picked late in their two-week harvest period.

I have yet to try a Criterion. Criterion was discovered as a chance seedling near Parker, Washington. The variety's genetic mix includes Red Delicious, Yellow Delicious, and Winter Banana. It was introduced in 1973.

The flesh is notably crisp, firm, and juicy. Criterion tastes mild and sweet, with a touch of tartness, and good aroma suffuses it all. This variety can be recommended for all kitchen uses, including drying. Following the October harvest, the fruit will keep its quality for some months.

Winesaps have been a staple for years in our kitchen. Winesaps is the distillation of a crisp fall day. The apple has character-too much character for some. Beneath its sturdy skin, the yellow flesh is firm, toothsome, and very juicy, with a powerful sweet-sour contrast and the characteristic winy flavor and aroma. Winesaps serves well in the kitchen, and its flavor carries over into sauce, pie, and cider. Note that its famously invigorating personality may be missing in areas where local climate or soil conditions are not favorable.

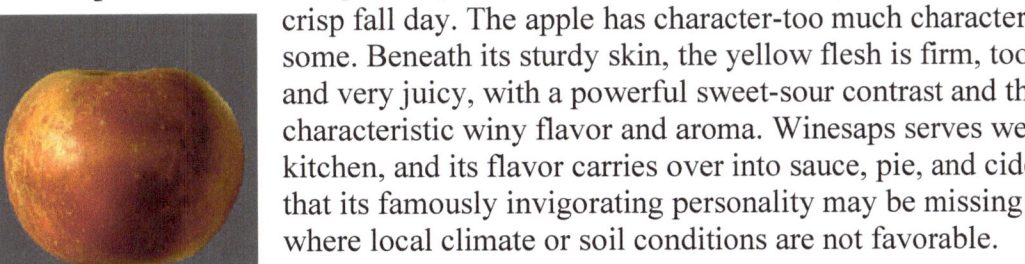

Winesaps is thought to have come from New Jersey. By 1817 it was recorded as an important cider apple in that state. Its popularity spread, and Winesap remained a major late-season apple until the mid-1900s, when controlled atmosphere storage made it possible to offer many varieties in its season. But Winesap continues to be widely grown, in spite of its relatively small size and competition from a milder offspring, Stayman.

Apples are ready for harvest between late September and early November and remain enjoyable for months. In blossom a row of Winesaps will glow pinker than most.

Here again is one of Carl's favorite apples, the Rome. Known also as simply Rome, this variety has a history that goes back to a fortuitous oversight. In the 1820s a tree planted along the northern bank of the Ohio River happened to send up a shoot from below the graft--from the part of the tree that is not supposed to bear fruit. Orchardists lop these unwanted shoots as routinely as they get haircuts. But this branch survived to bear splendidly colored fruit, and people began taking slips from it. The regionally famous tree was named for Rome Township, Ohio.

Sometime before the Civil War the waters rose up and washed the tree downriver. But by then Rome was well established. It continued to be grown more widely than many better-tasting varieties because of its size, conventionally handsome looks, and long shelf life.

Rome is a thick-skinned fruit that makes good eating but finds better use as a baker and in cider. The flesh, once you bite through to it, is crisp, firm, greenish white, and mildly tart.

Harvest is from late September into November. Beware of Romes that have become mealy and flavorless from storage.

Jonathan has come a long way since its discovery in Ulster County, New York, in the early 1800s. Within a hundred years it was the sixth best-selling apple in the United States, and it became Michigan's most popular variety. Jonathan's influence has been spread by a number of well-known crosses, most of them identifiable as family members because the names share the first four letters.

Jonathan can vary in flavor from mild to tart, depending on where it is grown. It has a spicy tang that some people also note in the apple's descendants. Beneath the thin, tough skin, the flesh is crisp, fine-textured, and juicy. It may be stained with red. This variety rates high for both eating fresh and cooking down into sauce, but it will not keep its shape when baked. Toss Jonathans into the hopper of a cider mill, and you'll retain something of their spicy character.

Jonathan ripens from mid-September through mid-October. The fruit does not keep particularly well.

Another favorite of mine is the Granny Smith. Granny Smith introduced American supermarket shoppers to the green apple. For a culture that had become unfamiliar with apples of that color, it came as a surprise that green does not necessarily mean unripe. Tart, Granny tends to be, but not sour and starchy.

The story goes that the first Granny Smith sprouted from a pile of apples tossed out by a southeast Australian named Mrs. Smith, back in 1868. This variety has succeeded commercially where other greens have not, for a few reasons. It is large. It is mild-flavored and has a good balance of tart and sweet. It is nearly as resilient as a tennis ball and holds up well in shipping. And Granny Smith will tolerate a half year of cold storage.

Brands of Granny applesauce and Granny apple juice are widely marketed. The apple can be baked as well. But eaten fresh, Granny is not an apple people tend to take to their hearts and name as their lifelong favorite. It's two-dimensional, lacking the hard-to-name qualities that make a fruit memorable.

The apples are harvested in October. As you sort through the piles of green fruits, keep in mind that paler Grannys, with a warmish cast, tend to be sweetest.

As I said, Carl loves the Golden Delicious apple. Golden Delicious is not related to the red variety of that name, although both were christened by Stark Brothers. This is a very easy apple to like. The skin is thin; the flesh, firm and crisp and juicy. Flavor and aroma are unmistakable, without being particularly assertive. Even the shape is somehow agreeable: large, tall, and conical, Golden Delicious strikes some cooks as too timid for the kitchen, but it can be used for pies and sauce with little or no sugar. Its distinctive aroma carries over into cider.

Golden Delicious began as a chance seedling, perhaps of Grimes Golden, on a farmer's hillside near Bomont, West Virginia. In 1914 Stark bought the tree for five thousand dollars, and protected its investment with a tall cage, complete with burglar alarm.

Apples ripen from mid-September through late October. The skin color can be a clue to quality; look for fruits that are pale yellow, not the chartreuse of an apple picked prematurely or the darker yellow that signals over ripeness. The skin is quick to shrivel if the apples are at room temperature, but Golden Delicious should keep well if refrigerated in the crisper or a plastic bag.

When I was a child, we mostly only saw and ate Red Delicious or Macintosh in our neighborhood. You are looking at the most controversial apple grown in North America. Red Delicious has become a symbol (a distinctively shaped logo, you could say) of the American apple. It represents the industry that has made it a stereotype. It also says much about a people who drop more of them in their shopping carts than any other apple.

Red Delicious is a marketer's ideal: as intensely red as the apple in Snow White, instantly recognizable, tall and wasp-waisted, and gorgeous even after the insides have gone to mush. And big. Riding on those qualities, the variety has pushed regional favorites aside. There is nothing imperialistic in this apple's genes, of course. It simply has been the lead player in our evolving notion of what an apple should be. The rise of Red Delicious has been called the victory of style over substance. Still, Big Red has its defenders, who point out that the original variety was a damned good apple. The skin is thick and bitter and has to be chewed vigorously. At its best the yellow flesh can be juicy, somewhat tart, and highly aromatic. This apple ranks close to the bottom when cooked. Harvest is in September, but the apples are sold year-round, so shop with skepticism. Delicious retains its cheerful good looks long after the flavor has departed.

McIntosh is the best-selling apple in the northeastern United States and in Canada. Unlike Red Delicious, the number one North American variety, it isn't the subject of snide remarks by apple aficionados.

John McIntosh, a farmer in Dundela, Dundas County, Ontario, Canada, gave his name to a talented cross between Fameuse and Detroit Red. The variety was introduced in 1870 and went on to much fame and much crossbreeding. McIntosh has lent its good genes to several well-known varieties, including Cortland, Empire, Macoun, and Spartan.

The original tree was badly scorched when a fire burned down the McIntosh farmhouse in 1894. But the old Mac limped on, yielding its last crop in 1908. It fell over two years later, and a stone memorial now marks the site.

The apple, in case you haven't visited your supermarket's produce section lately, has white, tender, crisp flesh that's spice, highly aromatic, and full of juice. The characteristic flavor carries over into sauce, but in the slices loses their shape. Macs are the principal cider apple in the Northeast.

Harvest is in September. Beware of McIntosh as winter wears on; the apples turn mealy if stored too long.

Newtown Pippin has been called the classic American apple. It holds the honor as the oldest commercially grown native variety in the United States. And it has a place in our lore, as the apple of George Washington's eye. Grafts found their way to Monticello, where Thomas Jefferson was eager to have the best and latest varieties.

The variety sprang from a seed in Newtown, Long Island. The original tree died when too many scions were cut from it for grafting. A greener version is known as Albemarle Pippin, named for the Virginia County, and Virginians claim it is more flavorful than Newtown.

Before Granny Smith invaded North America, Newtown was the best-appreciated green dessert apple. It continues to be enjoyed for a complexity that Granny lacks. Uncut, the apple may exhale a tangerine scent. The pale yellow flesh is crisp and tender, sweet on the tongue, and balanced by enough tartness. Some people detect a clean, pine like quality. One minor drawback is that slices brown rapidly. Newtown makes a thick sauce, excellent pies with body, and a particularly clear cider.

Apples are ready to be picked in October, when they have warmed to a pale greenish yellow. They continue to get sweeter and richer in flavor for the next five months.

 **Gravenstein has wandered around much of the world on its way to America.** It is thought to have originated in either Russia or Italy, before becoming established in Schleswig-Holstein, the neck of land that has been on both sides of the German-Danish border. So you may find the apple referred to as Russian, Italian, German, or Danish. Whatever its itinerary, the variety arrived in the United States in the late 1700s and continues to be grown commercially in California.

Gravenstein is thin-skinned and juicy, with sweetness and enough acid to make it interesting. It is an outstanding summer apple and an orchard antique deserving of its renewed interest. The Gravenstein personality carries through when cooking in pies and sauce and is noticeable in an all-Gravenstein cider.

The fruit is picked in late July and August. Be wary of Gravensteins still on the market in fall; their quality doesn't hold up in storage, and fruits may have become soft and mealy.

There are so many varieties of apples, that they could not be put here. I know of over 100 of them.

The last time we were in London, we stopped into Ye Olde Cheshire Cheese Pub at 5 Essex St. just off the Strand. Ye Olde Cheshire Cheese is one of the few pubs in London that can justify the *Ye Olde* in its name. Approached through a narrow alleyway (Wine Office Court) the Cheese beckons you into a bygone world. By the entrance a board lists the reigns of the 15 monarchs through which this grand old pub has survived. The dark wooden interior is an enchanting warren of narrow corridors and staircases, leading to numerous bars and dining rooms. There are so many even regulars get confused. The ground floor bar is the most interesting. This small room is very dark, with black timber paneled ceiling and walls. There's an open fire beneath a high mantle and above that the portrait of a waiter who started at the Cheese in 1829.

On a high shelf behind the bar are the leather- bound visitor's books. They contain the signatures of prime ministers, ambassadors and peers. Other patrons include Thackeray, Boswell, Dickens and Dr. Samuel Johnson, whose house is just around the corner.

The pub was rebuilt after the Great Fire (1666) destroyed its predecessor. A tavern is known to have stood here from at least the 16th century and a 13th century Carmelite Monastery once occupied this site. The vaulted cellars are thought to belong to that building.

This is a wonderful place and we met a lovely couple there and entered into a great evening of food and drink. The gentleman introduced us to real British Hard Cider, a wonderful drink. Our favorite was "Scrumpy Jack." From then on, the remainder of our week was trying out and enjoying all the varieties British Hard Ciders.

***Real cider* is essentially the fermented juice of the apple with nothing added and nothing taken away.** At the moment the majority of the cider sold in the UK is mostly made from imported apple concentrate, is full of artificial colorings, sweeteners, and preservatives, is filtered, is pasteurized to render it inert and is kept and served under carbon dioxide pressure. Don't assume that if it is served through a hand pump that it is real cider.

To protect traditional English varieties of cider and perry,* the Campaign for Real Ale (CAMRA) set up a sub-group, the Apple and Pear Produce Liaison Executive (APPLE). APPLE publishes the Good Cider Guide which lists pubs in Britain where real cider and perry are available. APPLE have defined two categories of real cider (and perry), anything which does not fall within these categories is not considered to be real cider (or perry*). * A light and fruity sparkling alcoholic drink similar to cider but made with pears rather than apples. **Waitrose Vintage English Perry** (500ml) is made in rural Herefordshire from specially selected English Perry pears, grown in this region since Norman times. It is fermented and matured in old oak vats, where it develops its special strength and unique flavor.

Category A

A definition agreed by APPLE to denote the very best of cider and perry, with nothing added or taken away.

Category A - must:

- not be pasteurized before or after fermentation
- not be filtered
- not receive enzyme treatment
- not contain preservatives or coloring
- not have the natural yeast replaced by a cultured yeast
- not have a nitrogen source added unless essential to start fermentation
- not be diluted
- only contain sweeteners if labeled *Medium* or *Sweet*, and then only if they are shown to be safe and do not affect the taste
- be produced from only freshly-pressed fruit, and
- not contain concentrate
- not contain extraneous carbon dioxide

Category B

Category A covers the majority of cider makers but only a small proportion of the total amount of cider made. A larger number of real ciders differ in some small respect from Category A ciders but are sufficiently authentic to be designated real cider since the taste and character of the cider is unaffected. These are Category B ciders.

Category B - must:

- not be entirely made from concentrate
- not contain extraneous carbon dioxide

North Americans use the term *sweet cider* to mean freshly-pressed apple juice, and *hard cider* to mean fermented apple juice, ie what in the UK would be termed cider.

Scrumpy

Scrumpy is a term often used to describe certain types of cider. It is one of those terms for which everyone has a definition and everyone's definition is different. Originally it was cider made from windfalls *(scrumps)*. For most people it means a rough, cloudy and unsophisticated cider. It is most often applied to young cider that which is only a few months old and has yet to undergo the maturation phase (including the malo-lactic fermentation). For other people, including some cider makers, it can mean the finest cider, from selected, better apples, slowly fermented and matured for longer than ordinary ciders.

When is it a cider and when an apple wine? This is a frequently asked question. There is no definitive answer to this. The best that can be said is that first of all apple wine falls outside of the definitions given above. Secondly, apple wine will almost always be made with dessert (sweet) apples. This materially affects the flavor of the finished drink. Cider apples contain high levels of tannins and significant amounts of malic acid. These are not found to significant levels in dessert apples. Therefore a cider has a sharpness (due to malic acid) and a bitterness (due to tannins) which is simply not found in apple wines. Commonly people will refer to the qualities that these components give to the cider as the *"bite"*. This is not apparent in apple wine. The final distinction is the alcohol content. Cider generally has an alcohol content which does not exceed (about) 8 percent by volume. Apple wines can commonly have higher alcohol contents. These wines will inevitably have been fermented using wine yeasts, not natural or ale yeasts, since only wine yeasts are tolerant to the high alcohol levels. The wine yeasts will impart their own flavor profile to the apple wine, moving it further away from a true cider. Note that in some countries the distinctions may be regulated by law on the basis of alcohol content alone.

Apple cider had been popular with the people of Great Britain going back to the time of the Celts. By the time the English had settled in America, the art of cider brewing was very well known to them due to centuries of consumption of apple cider.

During the Colonial Era, hard apple cider was by far the most popular alcoholic beverage in America. There were many reasons for the immense popularity of apple cider at that time.

First of all, apple cider is relatively easy to make. In addition to that, the early English colonists in America brought a great quantity of apple seed with them to plant in the New World resulting in an abundance of apple trees. By as early as 1629 there were already many apple orchards in Virginia and the Massachusetts Bay Colony. The reason for all this growing of apple trees was not to eat apples but to drink them in the form of hard cider.

Unlike many other alcoholic beverages, apple cider could be consumed at any time of the day. In fact, John Adams, second president of the United States, drank it regularly at breakfast to soothe his stomach. The fermentation of apple cider killed the bacteria in that drink which made it preferable to drinking well water in that era because water was often contaminated and therefore less healthy than apple cider.

Apple cider continued in its popularity well into the 1800s due in part to the efforts of the legendary Johnny Appleseed who planted many apple trees in the Midwest. As a result, apple cider brewing spread into that area of the country. By mid century, beer was a distant second to apple cider in popularity. However, soon a series of events took place which was to diminish the consumption of apple cider and make beer the most popular alcoholic beverage in America.

One of the factors that caused the gradual demise of hard apple cider is as the settlers moved further west; it became more difficult to grow apple trees in those arid regions. Later, as more people moved from the country to the city, there wasn't adequate transportation to deliver apple cider from the farms to the urban areas. Meanwhile, German beer with its faster fermentation process was introduced into America. The German immigrants also set up large sophisticated breweries for producing beer in great quantities while apple cider production remained limited to the small farms.

What ultimately led to the demise in the popularity of apple cider consumption was the Temperance movement. Because the Temperance movement was religiously based, many of the church going farmers gave up their drinking of apple cider. Many of them even went so far as to chop down the apple trees on their farms.

When Prohibition finally became the law, this marked the death knell for apple cider. Although beer staged a quick comeback following the repeal of Prohibition in 1933, apple cider brewing was effectively destroyed and remained only on a very few family farms for many years to come.

We personally are happy with the growing popularity of microbreweries in the 1990s, alcoholic apple cider is once again enjoying resurgence in popularity. Although apple cider is nowhere close to the popularity it enjoyed in the Colonial Era, the consumption of apple cider did double in just one year from 1995 to 1996 with renewed public interest in this brewing process considered to be so much a part of Americana.

As I have said, hard cider was once the drink of choice in early America. Today, sweet cider is enjoyed at harvest time and the hard stuff is making a comeback. The secret to making sweet or hard cider is the blending of apples at pressing time. A balanced blend of sweet and tart apples is needed. Hard or sweet, it's another great activity to enjoy at home.

Unfortunately for the home cider and apple wine maker, the addition of stabilizers to fresh pressed apple cider is becoming common. This is being done to extend the products shelf life. Cider which has been treated in this way will spoil before it ferments. The secret to making a great tasting cider is in the blending of apples prior to pressing. Making hard cider from a single type of apple will result in a bland drink with no real character.

Apple cider mills usually guard their secret recipes well. Basically, you use a blend of at least two apples mixed by weight at a ratio of 2:1. For sweet cider, use 2 parts sweet variety and one part tart. Reversing the mixture will make a dryer cider.

While the ratio remains the same, you can add more complexity and character by using more verities of apples. Our local supplier uses 6 varieties and that's all he's saying. Making hard cider is very much like making wine. Fresh pressed apple cider is fermented without the addition of any sugars. The starting gravity should be between 1.040 and 1.050. This will produce a dry cider with about 4.5% - 5% abv. The key to success is using fresh pressed cider that has not been treated in any way. Cider purchased at the super market will almost always contain preservatives and will rot before it will ferment. State and local laws require producers to treat apples with anti bacterial sprays prior to pressing and many require that stabilizers be added prior to sale. You must ask your supplier for wine or hard cider grade juice. Arrange to pick up your cider the day you will start to make it. The fresher the better!

Here is a recipe for making hard apple cider. Secure apple cider without preservative. Most apple cider for hard cider should be a blend of 3 or more varieties.

Fresh cider should be in clean containers. Wooden barrels make the best hard cider as the wood breathes and gives the cider proper aging.

To the cider add 1lb. of sugar per gallon for a dry hard cider (not sweet) or 1 1/2 lbs. for a sweet drink. Honey can be substituted for sugar on a pound per pound basis. Sugar and honey should be dissolved by warming some cider and mixing the sugar and honey until completely dissolved; then mixes with the cider.

Natural yeast in the juice will ferment the sugar to alcohol. Yeast need not be added, although it can without any problem. Some fermentation processes call for killing all the yeast in the pure cider with sulfur dioxide, waiting 24 hours and then adding wine yeast. For the homeowner this is not necessary.

Put air lock on container and keep at 60-70F for a couple of months. Lower temperatures take longer for product to change from sugar to alcohol.

After 2 months the juice should be decanted off (siphoned out of the container), the container washed, and the juice put back into the container. Do not use siphon hose closer than 4" from bottom of container as this is where all the sediment is resting.

After decanting, store at 40 - 60F in a wooden barrel and wait for proper aging -- 6 months to 6 years, depending upon desires.

Once juice is in container, the container cannot be moved as it will put sediment back into solution, and the results are a cloudy product.

Beet, grape, raspberry juice, etc. can be added for color.

Raisins can be added for sugar.

If cider is made in a 50-gallon wooded barrel, and you plan to draw it off over a 6-month period, a sulfur dioxide dispensing bung should be put on top bung hole once barrel is in use. This keeps the air space germ free and prevents off taste on the last used product.

For the average person making hard cider, glass or plastic gallons or five gallon jugs, or clean wooden barrels, are satisfactory. An air lock is needed to keep air out and let gas produced by the reaction escape. This can be done by purchasing an air lock from wine makers supply merchants. Another method is to drill a hole in the bottle stopper, insert a plastic tube that fits tightly, and put the other end of the tube in a container of water. This will let the gas bubble out and keep air or oxygen from getting in.

At one point in my life, when I was about 19 years old, I lived across the street from an apple cider vinegar factory. What an amazing scent was in the air every fall. There are lots of health opinions regarding apple cider vinegar, apple cider vinegar diets, and apple cider vinegar tablets or capsules.

Apple cider vinegar is a solution of acidic acid produced by fermentation of apples. It consists of acid, water, and only relatively small quantities of minerals. Although, it does contain a fair amount of pectin, which has recently been identified as lowering cholesterol and may be the secret behind it is fat burning effects.

The use of apple cider vinegar for the relief of arthritic stiffness and as a treatment for sore throats, acne, and other skin problems, high blood pressure, headaches, dandruff, sunburn, and elevated cholesterol levels has been around for ages.

There have been claims to the effect that the ancient Egyptians who used apple cider vinegar for weight loss created the apple cider vinegar diet. Claims have been made that apple cider vinegar works as an aid in weight loss and fat burning. However, there is no substantial or believable scientific evidence to support this claim. During the diet craze of the 1970's, proponents claimed that somehow a combination of apple cider, kelp, vitamin B-6, and lecithin tricked the body's metabolism into burning fat faster.

Today, the apple cider vinegar diet is back along with its many claims. This time, they are saying that to lose weight, take one, two, or three teaspoons of apple cider vinegar before every meal, starting with one teaspoon and then working up to two or three. Taking more than three teaspoons supposedly does not lead to better results. Probably more than three teaspoons is beyond what any dieter could reasonably stomach anyway. The only dieting advice you get with this "diet" is to eat moderate portions at meals, avoid snacking, and wait for the apple cider vinegar to reduce your hunger and food cravings.

So how does the apple cider vinegar figure into all of this effectively? Simply stated, it does not. Skip the apple cider vinegar if you want to lose weight and just reduce your food intake and increase your exercise.

Just consider the following when thinking about apple cider vinegar; it contributes to healthy veins, blood vessels and arteries. Apple cider vinegar has extraordinary potassium content and beneficial malic acid. When purchasing cider vinegar, it should have fuzzy sediment (mother), on the bottom, proving that the vinegar is still in the live fermentation stage. Cider vinegar is used in salad dressings and to spice up veggie juice mixtures. A tablespoon of cider vinegar and honey in hot water is a tasty health drink.

Apple Cider Vinegar Cucumbers
    Cucumbers
    Apple cider vinegar
    Sugar

Pack clean and dry cucumbers into a 1 gallon jug. Cover with apple cider vinegar and let set 6 weeks. Drain off vinegar and slice cucumbers into pint jars, alternating layers with sugar (takes a lot). When sugar has melted it should form liquid to cover. If not, add more sugar. Seal and enjoy.

Nothing beats Mom's Apple Pie

Pastry for two-crust 9-inch pie
6 Golden Delicious apples, peeled, cored, and thinly sliced
1/4 cup sugar
2 tablespoon flour
1 teaspoon vanilla extract
1/2 teaspoon cinnamon
1/4 teaspoon ground ginger
1/8 teaspoon ground mace
2 tablespoons butter or margarine
Cream or whole milk

1) Heat oven to 425 degrees F. Line a 9-inch pie pan with half the pastry. In large bowl, combine apples, sugar, flour, vanilla, cinnamon, ginger, and mace; toss well to blend. Transfer apple mixture to pastry-lined pie pan and dot with butter.

2) Cover apple filling with remaining pastry; pinch together edges of bottom and top crust to seal. Brush top crust with cream or milk; cut several slits to vent steam. Bake 20 minutes. Reduce oven heat to 375 degrees F and bake 30 to 35 minutes or until apples are tender.

In the cookie department, here are some good recipes.

Apple Cookies

1 1/2 cups of shredded unpeeled apple
1/4 cup of unsweetened apple juice
1/2 cup of granulated sugar
3/4 cup of dried cranberries or raisins
1 large egg
1/2 cup of packed brown sugar
1 teaspoon of vanilla extract
1/4 cup of vegetable oil
1 cup of unbleached all purpose flour
1/2 cup of rye flour
1 1/2 cups of quick cooking multigrain cereal
1 teaspoon of baking powder
1 teaspoon of baking soda
2 teaspoons of pumpkin pie spice

Preheat your oven to 350ºF. and coat 2 baking sheets with nonstick cooking spray. Combine the shredded apple, apple juice, granulated sugar, and cranberries. Set aside. Beat the egg, brown sugar, vanilla, and oil with an electric mixer until smooth. Add the shredded apple mixture and stir it into the batter by hand. Add the flours, cereal, baking powder, baking soda, and pie spice and stir into the batter by hand. Let the batter sit for about 5 minutes to absorb all of the liquid. Drop the batter by rounded teaspoonfuls about 2 inches apart onto the baking sheets and bake for 10 to 12 minutes or until the cookies are lightly browned. Cool on a wire rack. Repeat until all of the cookies are baked. Makes 60 cookies

Apple Cookies 2

1 1/2 cup of brown sugar
1/2 cup of shortening
1 egg
2 cups of flour
1 teaspoon of soda
1/2 teaspoon of salt
1 teaspoon of cinnamon
1 teaspoon of cloves
1 teaspoon of nutmeg

1 cup of chopped apples, peeled
1 cup of raisins
1 cup of chopped nuts
1/4 cup of milk

Sift together flour, soda, salt and spices. Cream together sugar and shortening. Add egg; beat well. Add flour mixture alternately with milk. Stir until smooth. Add apples, raisins and chopped nuts. Drop by teaspoon onto baking sheet. Bake at 400°F. until light brown.

Apple Oat Sesame Cookies

3/4 cup all-purpose flour
3/4 cup whole wheat flour
1/2 cup quick cooking oats
1/4 cup sesame seeds
1/4 cup sugar
1 teaspoon cinnamon
1 teaspoon baking powder
1/2 teaspoon baking soda
1/2 teaspoon nutmeg
1/4 teaspoon salt
1 1/2 cups finely chopped Golden Delicious apples
1/2 cup honey
1/2 cup vegetable oil
1/3 cup milk
1 large egg
3/4 cup golden raisins (optional)

1.) Heat oven to 375 degrees F. In large bowl, mix flours, the oats, sesame seeds, sugar, cinnamon, baking powder, baking soda, nutmeg, and salt. Stir in apples.

2.) In small bowl, beat together honey, oil, milk, and egg; add to oat mixture and stir until combined. Fold in raisins, if desired. Drop by tablespoonfuls onto ungreased cookie sheets. Bake 10 to 12 minutes or until lightly browned. Transfer cookies to wire rack and cool.

One of my favorite deserts was often made by the late Hazel Wright.

Apple Crisp

4 large apples

1/2 cup brown sugar
1 cup flour
3/4 cup white sugar
1 tsp. cinnamon
1/4 tsp. salt
2 Tbs. melted butter
1 egg
1/2 cup water

Preheat the oven to 375 degrees.

Then, peel, core and slice the apples. Put the apples in a bowl and mix in 1/2 cup brown sugar.
In a separate bowl, using a fork, mix together 1 cup flour, 3/4 cup sugar, 1 teaspoon cinnamon, and 1/4 teaspoon salt.

In another bowl beat together 1 egg, 2 tablespoons melted butter and 1/2 cup water. Add them to the dry ingredients. You've now made the topping.

Put the apples in baking dish and pour the topping over them.
Bake in the oven for 30 - 40 minutes. When it's done the apples should be soft and the topping golden and crisp.

Remove from oven and let cool.

Here is an **Apple & Raisin Almond Crisp** Easier than pie . . .
Yield: 6 - 8 Servings
Time:
25 minutes to assemble
45 minutes to bake
Total Time: 70 minutes
Ingredients:

Ingredients

1 cup raisins

6 large (3 lbs) Granny Smith apples

1 Tbsp & 1/2 cup flour

1/3 cup sugar

1 & 1/2 tsp cinnamon, divided

Pinch of salt

1 box (7oz) Almond Paste

1 cup quick cooking oats

1/2 cup light brown sugar

1 stick (8 Tbsp) soft butter, cut into small pieces
Equipment:
2 quart casserole dish or deep bowl Box grater Pastry cutter, optional

Directions. 1 Preheat oven to 375 F.

Place raisins in a saucepan and just barely cover with water. Bring to a boil and turn off heat. Cover and set aside.

Peel, core and slice apples into 1/4" pieces. Place in a casserole dish or deep bowl that is oven proof.

In a small bowl mix together 1 Tbsp flour, sugar, 1 tsp cinnamon, and a pinch of salt together. Sprinkle over apples and set aside.

Grate the almond paste into a medium bowl. Add the remaining flour and cinnamon, oats, brown sugar and butter. Using a pastry cutter, or 2 knives, cut in the butter until mixture has the texture of small crumbs.

Drain the raisins and add to apples. Toss together to mix well.

Top with almond paste / oat mixture and bake for 45 minutes. If crisp is browning too quickly, loosely tent the top (do not wrap) with aluminum foil. Continue to cook until apples bubble and top turns a dark golden color.

Cool for 15 minutes before serving.

I can remember the late Dick Greene making the most delicious Baked Apples

Prep and Cook Time: 1 hour

Ingredients:
4 crisp red apples
2 TBS fresh lemon juice
2 cups water
Filling
½ cup honey or maple syrup
½ cup raisins
½ cup chopped walnuts
1 tsp cinnamon

Directions:

Preheat oven to 350

Core apples using a melon baller leaving the bottom of apple so they hold the stuffing. Combine lemon juice and water, and place apples in it as you complete coring them.

Mix stuffing ingredients together and fill cavity of apples.

Place apples in a baking dish with about 1 cup of the lemon water in the bottom of the dish. Bake uncovered for about 50-60 minutes depending on size of apples, until they are tender. Drizzle juice from bottom of pan over apples and serve hot.

We have covered a lot about apples and have not even touched the surface of apple information, history, and recipes. I hope this chapter makes you want to do a lot with apples, if nothing else, eat them or at least once a day.

Better still, plant a couple of apple trees in your yard. Someone in the future will thank you for them. Who knows where it will even take you. Planting a small orchard and expanding on it every year is a grand investment toward retirement.

Please will always be eating apples and perhaps you are the right person to start their own apple orchard business.

Chapter 14

Starting a Garden is like having a Baby!

Yes, it is great to see all those gardens, to picture the harvests, to consider and test the recipes from those harvests. However, starting a garden IS like having a baby because once you start you need to be responsible for that garden.

It needs to be tended to. Watered, hoed, weeded, trimmed, turned over, pruned, dug up, replanted, cut back, thinned out and all the other little things that most of us never think about prior to starting a garden or an orchard.

You will become its care giver, a gardener or orchard man, gentleman farmer, serf, peasant or whatever you want to call it and if the bug bites you, you will probably lay out more money than you intended.

You will need rakes, hoes, shovels, wagons, wheel barrows, pruners, seeds, plants, mulch, fertilizer, gardening gloves, hoses to say nothing of the myriad of things all garden centers lure us with.

You might decide you cannot live without a compactor or how about a nice rototiller since that will do all the work for you? I know, been there/done that! The operative word here is WORK!

You might want to remember that gardening shows are like cooking shows such as Emeril who has an army of helpers running around in the invisible background making him make it all look so easy.

Well, unless you have some secret that I don't know about consider yourself an army of one. You may just luck out with a spouse who likes gardening as much as you do or dream kids that cannot wait to go out and weed.

Also, unless you do some serious planning in the beginning you are going to have continued work. I find it harder and harder each spring and summer to find help at even $8.00 an hour to help in my garden.

You may need to hire help when you go on vacation to water those containers or do the weeding while you are gone.

Consider doing some serious planning in order to deal with this global warming. Consider drip watering apparatus and self watering containers. Sit down with a pencil and paper and write down your budget at the top of the pad and then stick to it.

Do some research on the weather in your area for the past 5 or 10 years and see if you can spot the cycles you might have to deal with.

Decide whether or not 2 or 4 tomato plants will give you want you want or do you need 2 or 4 long rows that will take a lot more work to maintain.

Realize that you might not be able to be a "week end" gardener especially if you have a day job. You might be too tired when you come home after a day in the office or whatever to want to go out and play in the dirt.

You might think you have a black thumb and if you really feel you do, then don't start a garden of any kind. You were not born with a black thumb. You just did not have the time or perhaps resources to devote to whatever it is you killed off.

Still not discouraged? Let's get on with it then.

Make sure you design your garden on paper first.

Then make a list of what you want to plant and make sure it will grow in your zone. Something you saw and fell in love with on your last trip to Florida will not survive in Michigan!

Make sure you wear a gardening hat and make sure you get out there early in the a.m. because you do not want a sun stroke thinking you can get out there and do your gardening work mid day.

Maybe you might want to consider other types of gardening such as:

Indoor gardening is concerned with the growing of houseplants within a residence or building, in a conservatory, or in a greenhouse. Indoor gardens are sometimes incorporated as part of air conditioning or heating systems.

Water gardening is concerned with growing plants adapted to pools and ponds. Bog gardens are also considered a type of water garden. These all require special conditions and considerations. A simple water garden may consist solely of a tub containing the water and plant(s).

Container gardening is concerned with growing plants in any type of container either indoors or outdoors. Common containers are pots, hanging baskets, and planters. Container gardening is usually used in atriums and on balconies, patios, and roof tops.

Gardening is the practice of growing flowering plants, vegetables, and fruits. Residential gardening most often takes place in or about a residence, in a space referred to as the garden. Although a garden typically is located on the land near a residence, it may also be located in a roof, in an atrium, on a balcony, in a windowbox, or on a patio or vivarium.

Remember when you start that you intend to be a gardener, not a farmer! Keep it small in the beginning. Should you be lucky and have a bumper crop think about what you are going to do with it since it is more than likely your friends might have bumper crops that year also. The produce usually comes in all at once and that means canning or freezing your harvest.

You might want to start a community garden if you have the room and allow people to have small spaces to grow flowers and vegetables in exchange for a small share of their bounty. A sort of reverse "share cropper"!

Find out if there is a local gardening club in your area and join it. They will load you up with free plants usually.

Contact a county extension officer in your area to help with finding out what kind of soil you have and what you will need to amend it.

Before you haul in a truck load of manure from your local farmer find out if they feed organic feed to their live stock and beware of E-Coli that may be harbored in any manure you might obtain.

Be aware of the fact that there is a difference in weeds such as annual and perennial just like flowers and perennial weeds usually come back every year if you spent a good deal of time weeding simply because most of them spread through their root systems.

You might want to consider raised beds and I don't mean the kind that are only 8" high since you still have to bend over. So how about this type that Carl built for me.

Know which direction your gardens face. Do you get the sun all day? Where is the shade? Which parts are exposed to the wind? Do you have any walls or fences to protect your plants?

Remember to try to plant as many perennials as you can because they can flourish for years - not like annuals and bi-annuals which are time consuming and need lots of attention.

Get a soil testing kit and discover if you have alkaline or acid soil? An easy way to tell is from the color of a hydrangea should you have any in your garden. These plants will turn pink or blue depending on the acidity of the soil.

When planting trees, shrubs or containers of plants brought home from the nursery remember to dig a hole that's wide enough for the roots to spread out BUT not too deep.

Weeds will be your enemy and their seeds are spread by wind, birds and their own root systems. You can pull them out or spray them which are expensive or even perhaps harmful or you can hoe, hoe, hoe which is the best way.

Go to the library and get some good gardening books out during the winter months.

In the event, at this point, you are still ready to make a garden then remember to

"Tread the Earth lightly", and in the meantime… may your day be filled with….

Peace, Light and Love,

Arlene Wright-Correll

Arlene's Gardening Hat©

www.ingramcontent.com/pod-product-compliance
Lightning Source LLC
Chambersburg PA
CBHW041519220426
43667CB00002B/38